Cambridge Elements

Elements in Women Theatre Makers
edited by
Elaine Aston
Lancaster University
Melissa Sihra
Trinity College Dublin

ADAPTATIONS IN THE LIFE AND WORK OF DIRECTOR TIAN QINXIN

Yuan Li
Guangdong University of Foreign Studies

Shaftesbury Road, Cambridge CB2 8EA, United Kingdom

One Liberty Plaza, 20th Floor, New York, NY 10006, USA

477 Williamstown Road, Port Melbourne, VIC 3207, Australia

314–321, 3rd Floor, Plot 3, Splendor Forum, Jasola District Centre,
New Delhi – 110025, India

Cambridge University Press is part of Cambridge University Press & Assessment,
a department of the University of Cambridge.

We share the University's mission to contribute to society through the pursuit of
education, learning and research at the highest international levels of excellence.

www.cambridge.org
Information on this title: www.cambridge.org/9781009583145

DOI: 10.1017/9781009583152

© Yuan Li 2026

This publication is in copyright. Subject to statutory exception and to the provisions
of relevant collective licensing agreements, no reproduction of any part may take
place without the written permission of Cambridge University Press & Assessment.

When citing this work, please include a reference to the DOI 10.1017/9781009583152

First published 2026

A catalogue record for this publication is available from the British Library

*A Cataloging-in-Publication data record for this Element is available from the
Library of Congress*

ISBN 978-1-009-58314-5 Hardback
ISBN 978-1-009-58317-6 Paperback
ISSN 2634-2391 (online)
ISSN 2634-2383 (print)

Cambridge University Press & Assessment has no responsibility for the persistence
or accuracy of URLs for external or third-party internet websites referred to in this
publication and does not guarantee that any content on such websites is, or will remain,
accurate or appropriate.

For EU product safety concerns, contact us at Calle de José Abascal, 56, 1°, 28003
Madrid, Spain, or email eugpsr@cambridge.org

Adaptations in the Life and Work of Director Tian Qinxin

Elements in Women Theatre Makers

DOI: 10.1017/9781009583152
First published online: February 2026

Yuan Li
Guangdong University of Foreign Studies
Author for correspondence: Yuan Li, yl3243150@gmail.com

Abstract: This Element examines Tian Qinxin (1969–), one of the most prominent theatre directors in contemporary China, and her significant contribution to the development of mainstream Chinese theatre in the twenty-first century. Since her debut productions in the late 1990s, Tian has cultivated a distinctive directorial style, marked by a syncretic fusion of Western and traditional Chinese theatrical elements. While she has worked across a variety of genres, her primary focus has been on stage adaptations. Adaptation is not only a defining feature of her theatrical practice but also a central aspect of her professional life, where shifting political and cultural contexts necessitate her "performance" of various expressions of both femininity and masculinity. Tian's remarkable adaptability enables her to skillfully navigate the evolving landscape of Chinese theatre, the demands of state cultural policy, and the requirements of the commercial theatre sector.

Keywords: Chinese contemporary theater, Tian Qinxin, adaptation, playful theatricals, main melody plays

© Yuan Li 2026

ISBNs: 9781009583145 (HB), 9781009583176 (PB), 9781009583152 (OC)
ISSNs: 2634-2391 (online), 2634-2383 (print)

Contents

	Introduction	1
1	Adapting by Performing Gender	3
2	Adapting Works by Chinese Women Novelists	21
3	Adapting Chinese Classics and Shakespeare	43
	Conclusion	62
	References	65

Introduction

Tian Qinxin, born in Beijing in 1969, graduated from the Directing Department of the Central Academy of Drama. She currently serves as President of the National Theatre of China (NTC) and is acknowledged as "one of the most important directors in the twenty-first century" (Chen 2023: 77).

Historically, Chinese theatre (like theatre in the rest of the world) has been dominated by male playwrights, directors, and producers, with women confined to acting roles until the 1990s. At that time, several talented Chinese female directors and playwrights emerged, most of whom produced a small number of works. In that regard, Tian stands out as an exception, having established her status as a leading director through two decades of consistent, vigorous creative work.

From 1999 to 2022, Tian's impressive portfolio includes directing seventeen spoken dramas, three television dramas, two musicals, and two traditional Chinese operas. She is the first woman director to be employed by NTC and became its first female President in 2020. Her professional trajectory illuminates the development of Chinese mainstream theatre in the twenty-first century.

Since her debut productions at the end of the 1990s *(Breaking Wrist*, 1997; *The Field of Life and Death*, 1999), Tian has developed a signature directing style, characterized by syncretism and hybridity, while adapting to the changing landscape of Chinese theatre by negotiating between the requirements of state cultural policy, the preferences of the market, and the values guiding her artistic pursuits. She has explored various genres, including spoken dramas, television dramas, musicals, and traditional Chinese operas, with a primary focus on adapting works for the stage. Her adaptations can be categorized into three kinds: adaptations of significant works by modern Chinese women novelists; adaptations of the Chinese classics; and renditions of two plays by Shakespeare. These adaptations testify to her ability to cross the boundaries between the public and the private, the past and the present, the personal and the political, and the traditional and the revolutionary (Yan 2010: 519). Adaptation is not only a key characteristic of her work on stage but also in Tian's everyday life, where shifting political and artistic contexts call for her to present different traits of femininity and masculinity.

Although Tian's directing has received some scholarly attention in China, there is no extensive study of her work. In the West, she has received far less critical attention than her male peers, such as directors Meng Jinghui and Yu Rongjun.[1] This Element aims to analyze Tian's work as a director and account

---
[1] The few studies of Tian include: Chou, Katherine Hui-ling. 2016. "Staging a New Venture: Tian Qinxin's *The Yellow Storm* and the Policy Change on the Huaju Industry in

for the important role she has played in the twenty-first-century development of China's mainstream theatre, an undertaking that involves situating her theatre in shifting political, gender, and theatrical contexts.

Comprised of three main sections, this Element begins with an analysis of Tian's training, early career, and eventual rise to prominence as the President of the NTC and as a member of the Chinese People's Political Consultative Conference (CPPCC), a professional trajectory that also illuminates the development of Chinese mainstream theatre in the twenty-first century (Section 1). Adopting a biographical approach, Section 1 traces Tian's path to directing and examines how she modulates gender presentation – at times adopting masculine attire or a more male presentation, at others a distinctly feminine presentation. This discussion is historicized within the longer Chinese tradition of female gender disguise in classical opera and, in everyday life, among modern women revolutionaries who strategically adopted masculine styles. I argue that Tian's gendered self-presentation in the early twenty-first century operates along two key dimensions. First, it is pragmatic and contained, resonating with the archetype of the warrior woman in traditional theatre and with socialist ideals of working women in the 1950s and 1960s. Second, her shifting embodiment retains a playful quality that she links to classical performance practices, in which actors move with ease across roles and codes. Sections 2 and 3 examine Tian's adaptation strategies and her distinctive style that hybridizes Western and Chinese theatre-making. Section 2 focuses on her theatrical renderings of works by Chinese women novelists (Xiao Hong, Aileen Chang, and Lilian Lee Pik-Wah), considering her adaptation strategies and the sociopolitical and cultural contexts of the works she adapts. Section 3 explores her adaptations of classic and modern Chinese plays, including how she blends traditional themes with contemporary perspectives, and her use of localization strategies in adapting plays by Shakespeare.

Directing in the mainstream, Tian has had to navigate the three genres that have dominated the stage since the early 2000s: main melody (a form of propaganda drama), experimental, and commercial theatre. In this regard, analysis will demonstrate her capacity for blending and reinvigorating these categories, but in ways that also have to fall in line with state policy and commercial success. From the nationalism prevalent at the close of the twentieth century to the individualist expressions of desire and frustration of the early

---

China." In Ruru Li ed., *Staging China : New Theatres in the Twenty-First Century*. New York: Palgrave Macmillan, 159–76; Zhang, Ranran. 2019. "Nationality and Universality: The Rewrite of *Madam White Snake* under Globalization in Tian Qinxin's Play *Green Snake*." *Journal of Arts and Humanities* 8.11: 35–9; Li, Yuan and Tim Beaumont. 2022. "Salome Complex and The Discourses of Sentiment in *Hurricane, the Life of Tian Han*." *Asian Theatre Journal* 39.2:241–66.

twenty-first century, and the ongoing comparisons between China and the West in the past and the present, Tian's theatrical adaptations speak directly to her contemporary audience, engaging with both public ideologies and private emotions.

1 Adapting by Performing Gender

From photos and interviews of Tian across different stages of her life, one can observe a fascinating evolution in her appearance and mannerisms.[2] She moves from a feminine presentation in her early twenties – signaled by long black hair – to a more masculine, assertive appearance with a crew cut in her thirties and forties, and later, in her fifties, to an elegant style frequently characterized by traditional Chinese dress. This visual and stylistic transformation raises intriguing questions about the development of gender in her life and work. How did these changes occur, and what do they signify? Moreover, how are the gender dynamics Tian navigates in her professional life reflected in her theatrical adaptations and productions? By exploring these questions, we can gain deeper insights into Tian's artistic vision and the broader cultural contexts that shape her work. Her gender identity and expression are not fixed throughout her life, but rather, develop and transform at different points.

A useful analogy is Mulan, the legendary heroine of the Northern Dynasties (fourth to sixth centuries), renowned for disguising herself as a man, who endures in fiction and on stage.[3] In the classic ballad and many operatic retellings, Mulan's departure for war and her return to domestic femininity are framed not as rebellion but as compliance with filial and social norms. Read alongside this tradition, Tian's own path can be understood as a cyclical performance of gender – moving from femininity to masculinity and back to femininity. As Judith Butler has argued, gender is not an innate identity but a performative effect, produced through repeated acts that conform to social expectations (Butler 1999: 43–4). Each of Tian's transitions aligns with prevailing ideological demands: first conforming to the masculine norms deemed necessary for a director, and later embracing the feminine role prescribed for

---

[2] See "Extraordinary Women (special feature)" n.d. NetEase Lady (163.com). https://lady.163.com/special/sense/extraordinary_women07.html, accessed on July 1, 2025; "Baidu Baijiahao article" n. d. Baidu Baijiahao (baidu.com). https://baijiahao.baidu.com/s?id=1793463750098220784&wfr=spider&for=pc, accessed on July 1, 2025.

[3] "The Ballad of Mulan" (*Mulan ci* 木兰辞) is an anonymous *yuefu* poem of the Northern Dynasties (4th–6th centuries), preserved in Guo Maoqian's *Yuefu shiji* 《乐府诗集》 (*Collection of Music Bureau Poems*, c. twelfth century). It relates how Hua Mulan, to spare her ageing father, dons male attire, serves with distinction in the army for twelve years, then declines imperial honours and returns home to resume her female identity. The tale has enjoyed a long afterlife in Chinese drama and opera and continues to shape modern stage and screen adaptations.

a woman leader, thereby symbolizing her integration into the establishment. In this context, as with Mulan, Tian's gender shifts are rewarded rather than punished. Her performance of gender, then, is marked less by subversion than by adaptation and compliance.

Yet Tian is not reducible to the feudal template: Her trajectory is marked by agency and self-fashioning. As a contemporary Chinese woman, she acts within conditions shaped first by state-led women's emancipation in the 1950s to 1970s and later by marketization and the rise of the cultural industries in the 1990s. These circumstances enabled her pursuit of professional eminence. On the one hand, her enactments of gender display traits of what Butler calls performativity, in that they cater to dominant ideological expectations and reproduce mainstream norms. On the other hand, Tian's practice has a consciously theatrical dimension. Drawing on *xiqu* (Chinese theatre/opera) traditions of playacting and masquerade, she treats gender as a repertoire of roles to be assumed, set aside, and recomposed according to the demands of her work. Unlike Butler's concept of performativity, which is not a singular voluntary act but the reiteration of norms that constitute the subject, Tian's gender performance involves a more deliberate enactment akin to playing a role on stage. Her presentations are not merely accommodative but also strategic and pragmatic, serving as tools for directing and leadership. Like an actor shifting parts, she moves fluidly between gendered personae, an agility that also sustains her artistic vision.

1.1 Early Training, Influences, and the Path to Directing

Tian Qinxin was born into a middle-class family in Beijing in 1969. Her father, who had a military background and a passion for the arts, and her mother, a professional painter and art teacher at the Affiliated High School of the Central Academy of Fine Arts, created a culturally enriched environment at home, regularly hosting painters and artists. However, Tian reflects in one of her interviews that she had a rather lonely childhood because her parents were often busy with their work (Zhao 2015). Despite her initial interest in painting, she was sent to boarding schools from the age of five and grew increasingly detached from her parents. She spent four years at the Shichahai Sports School learning gymnastics. According to Tian, this was a very unpleasant experience, as she was constantly ridiculed by fellow students due to her clumsiness (Zhao 2015).

At the age of eleven, Tian was sent to another boarding school specializing in *jingju* (Peking opera). Traditional Chinese opera adheres to distinctive typographic conventions, encompassing diverse musical modes, tune patterns, and character role designations, including Mo (male characters, secondary roles),

Dan (female characters), Jing (painted faces, usually powerful male figures like warriors, gods, or demons), and Chou (clowns). As a result, young students are assigned specific roles from the outset. In this *jingju* school, Tian was trained as a *daomadan* (literally, knife, horse, and woman), a female martial role involving onstage combat. Tian later reflected on her time at the opera school as miserable due to severe stage fright. Reflecting on her early years at these boarding schools, Tian recalled that she grew increasingly introverted, keeping her distance from others, and found solace in the theatre. Living in Beijing, a city rich in theatrical activities, she would ride her bicycle to various parts of the city to watch plays (Yang 2012). Despite these challenging experiences, Tian's seven years at the opera school fostered a deep appreciation for theatre and traditional Chinese performance arts. This influence is evident in her directing career, where her approaches to casting, stage design, and role portrayal reflect her background in traditional Chinese theatre.

As she grew older, Tian was finally able to make her own decisions and, driven by her desire to be the person behind the stage rather than on it, applied to the directing department of the Central Academy of Drama in 1991. In 1993, Tian spent some time in England, immersing herself in London's theatre scene. She also visited Stratford, the birthplace of Shakespeare. In one of her interviews, she mentioned spending seven pounds on a statue of Shakespeare, which still sits in her room to this day (Zhao 2015). This early admiration for Shakespeare perhaps laid the foundation for her later adaptations of *King Lear* and *Romeo and Juliet*. However, Tian also confessed that her time in England made her acutely aware of her Chinese identity (Zhao 2015). This reinforced her attachment to Chinese culture, and her adaptations of Shakespeare's plays are distinctly Sinicized.

Sheila Melvin captures Tian's early temperament and sense of belated awakening: "Tian is resolutely unglamorous and self-deprecating, a self-described late bloomer who claims to have failed at everything in her youth, which included long, miserable stints in boarding schools for gymnastics and the Peking opera, and 'didn't wake up' until she was 26" (Melvin 2008). After graduating in 1995, Tian did not immediately pursue directing. Reeling from a failed relationship, she relocated to Shenzhen, where she spent two years working in advertising and recovering emotionally. During this time, she gradually rediscovered her love for theatre (Yang 2012). In 1997, she returned to Beijing and channeled her heartbreak into her debut play, *Breaking Wrist*, a modern retelling of a historical romance that she later described as offering closure for her first love (Yang 2012). The play premiered in April 1997 at the China Children's Theatre in Beijing, and on September 24, 1997, it also opened at the Beijing People's Art Theatre Studio Theatre It was a breakthrough success and drew the attention of Zhao Youliang (1944–2023), then president of the Central Experimental Theater (predecessor of the National Theater of China), who offered her a directing position after seeing the performance (Yang 2012). That offer launched her career in one of China's leading theatre companies. By 1999, she had staged her first major work, *The Field of Life and Death*, which inaugurated two decades of influential directorial work. As Tian notes, her early works were characterized by spontaneity and passion, reflecting her artistic vision (Zhou and Huang 2013). These include her debut work *Breaking Wrist* (1997) and subsequent plays such as *The Field of Life and Death* (1999) and *Hurricane* (2001) – a biographical play about Tian Han (1898–1968), one of the founding fathers of modern Chinese drama – as well as her adaptation of *The Orphan of Zhao* (2003) and Kong Shangren's classical Kunqu opera *The Peach Blossom Fan* (2006).

However, from the beginning of the twenty-first century, with the state adopting a policy of integrating theatre into the cultural industry, in her capacity as a director, Tian faced systemic pressure to increase box office sales. Consequently, her later theatrical adaptations reflect her efforts to balance artistic integrity with market demands, achieving significant success in mainstream Chinese theatre over the past twenty years. Featuring all-star casts and spectacular stage productions, these adaptations attained phenomenal box-office success. Her notable works in this phase include the adaptation of Eileen Chang's *Red Rose and White Rose* (2007), the Ming Dynasty-set rendition of Shakespeare's *King Lear* titled *Ming* (2008), *The Yellow Storm* (2010), adapted from a novel by Lao She (1899–1966), and *Green Snake* (2013), based on a novel by Lilian Lee Pik-Wah (1959–).

Since 2017, Tian's career has taken a new turn. She was selected as a member of the CPPCC (the National Committee of the CPPCC, which serves as an advisory body for government, legislative, and judicial organs and puts forward proposals on major political and social issues). In 2020, she was also appointed as the president of the National Theatre (NTC) of China. This official recognition by the central government granted her greater political and cultural capital. In this new position, Tian feels a sense of mission to tell more Chinese stories through her prestigious platform (Liu and Wei 2021). Her recent works include two major television cultural programs, *China in Stories* (2019–2021) and *China in Classics* (2021), coproduced by the NTC, CCTV Comprehensive Channel, and Creative Media. On October 1, 2021, the play *Live Broadcast of the Founding Ceremony*, which she wrote and directed, premiered at the National Centre for the Performing Arts. In October 2022, her directed play *Arts in the War of Resistance* also premiered at the National Centre for the Performing Arts. Drawing on her familiarity with historical narratives and infusing them with nationalistic sentiments, she has produced several plays in the "main melody" genre. This genre, often regarded as propaganda theatre, features "interesting and touching stories ranging from ancient China to revolutionary history, socialist development since 1949, and the achievements of economic reforms" (Li 2016: 55).

1.2 Performing Gender

Tian Qinxin has notably referred to herself as "shy and timid" in interviews (Yang 2012). But over the course of her career, she has grown into the formidable first woman director of the NTC and subsequently its leader, as well as a high-ranking woman cadre in the CPPCC. In this process, she has adapted to her changing professional roles by performing the gender traits most advantageous for each.

In her first transformation, Tian altered her feminine image to adopt a short-haired, masculine appearance, which often incited questions and curiosity. In an interview with the famous hostess Yang Lan,[4] Tian acknowledged the scarcity of women theatre directors and the fact that the rules of the game are predominantly set by men. She highlighted several practical problems she encounters as a director.

First, she noted, "When you look attractive, men need to look past your appearance and focus on what you're actually saying in order to work effectively. If your looks become a distraction, it can prevent them from overcoming their own gender biases, leading to less effective collaboration" (Yang 2012). Therefore, she explained, by assuming a more masculine look, she aimed to simplify her professional interactions, and ensure that "her female sexuality did not distract male actors." Second, there are technical challenges such as synthesis and stage setup, all of which must be completed within a short timeframe. Leading such a large team requires strong command and control abilities. Given her naturally shy and timid personality, adopting a more masculine appearance served as a protective shield, enabling her to be more assertive and effective as a director (Yang 2012). Her account rests on gender-essentialist assumptions and reinforces conventional gender dichotomies, thereby supporting the argument that she positions herself within traditional gender frameworks and adapts to them rather than subverts them (see Figure 1).

---

[4] Yang Lan is a prominent Chinese media entrepreneur, journalist, and television host, often referred to as the "Oprah of China." She has hosted numerous influential talk shows, including "Yang Lan One on One," where she has interviewed global leaders and cultural icons. Yang Lan is renowned for her work focusing on social and cultural issues and has been recognized as one of the most powerful women in Chinese media.

Figure 1 Tian Qinxin in *Yang Lan One on One* in 2012. Screenshot by the author from the interview "Tian Qinxin," *Yang Lan One on One*, hosted by Yang Lan, *Youku*, https://vo.youku.com/v_show/id_XNDU4MzY5MzIw.html. Accessed October 15, 2025. Screenshots labeled "by the author" are taken from publicly available video sources and reproduced under fair dealing for scholarly criticism and review.

As previously noted, Tian was greatly influenced by traditional Chinese opera due to her seven years of training and childhood immersion in theatres. She mentioned that the idea of her enactment as a man is inspired by Chinese traditional opera, which is characterized by a strong sense of theatricality and meta-theatricality. The traditional Chinese character for *xi* (drama and theatre) 戲, combines "虛" (illusion) and "戈" (weapon), underscoring the emphasis on impersonation and make-believe (Yang 2012). Among all the theatrical maneuvers on the Chinese stage, cross-dressing, with its thirteen-century-long tradition, stands out as one of the most prominent, sitting at the intersection of gender and performance. This practice illustrates that femininity and masculinity are constructs established through performance, rather than innate qualities defined as real or fake by nature (Li 2003: 6–7).

Historically, European theatre, beginning with classical Greece, excluded women from the stage, relying instead on male actors to perform female roles. It wasn't until the seventeenth century that women gradually began to appear on stage, though they were often objectified for the male audience's pleasure (Li 2003: 29). This exclusion of women, coupled with the cultural construction of "femininity" from a masculine perspective, and the asymmetry between male and female cross-dressing, contributed to a theatre environment where women were viewed as lesser performers. They were seen as playing themselves rather than creating roles, thus inspiring later feminist critiques of the use of women as mere symbols to be manipulated by male playwrights and actors (Ferris 1989: xi). This perspective posits that women, as theatrical signs, are passive and subject to male control (Li 2003: 30).

According to Siu Leung Li, *xiqu* (Chinese traditional opera) provides an alternative example of inclusive theatrical practice. Female performers have played a crucial role in the development of *xiqu* (opera and theatre) since the Yuan Dynasty (1206–1368 CE). Cross-gender role-playing has been widespread, with both men portraying women and women taking on male roles across the many regional subforms of *xiqu*. During this period, female actors often held leading roles on stage, frequently cross-dressing to play male characters. In the Ming (1368–1644) and Qing (1644–1911) periods, private troupes maintained by the gentry and public theatres prominently featured cross-dressing. These private troupes were mostly female, composed of young actresses performing in the refined Kunqu opera style, and theatre historians credit these women with significant contributions to the evolution of this opera form (Li 2003: 2).[5] However, the prevalence of all-male casting and female impersonation in public theatre, particularly in Peking opera, emerged after Emperor Qianlong's ban on actresses in Beijing in 1772 (Chou 1997: 131).[6]

Li argues that the widespread misconception in the West, that Chinese opera is primarily a male transvestite theatre, has been perpetuated by the success of David Henry Hwang's Broadway hit *M. Butterfly* (1989) and Chen Kaige's Palme d'Or-winning film *Farewell My Concubine* (1993) (Li 2003: 40). Both Li and Chou Hui-ling aim to correct this misunderstanding by emphasizing that female cross-dressing has a tradition as longstanding and consistent as male cross-dressing in the history of Chinese theatre. They trace this practice back to

---

[5] The Kunqu opera originated in the Jiangnan region of China during the late sixteenth century and evolved into a refined classical Chinese performing art over the next two hundred years. It is renowned for its poetic lyrics, melodious tunes, exquisite dances, and elegant, stylized performances.

[6] After the establishment of the Republic of China in 1911, the opera artist Yu Zhenting (1887–1938) petitioned the new government to lift the ban on women performers in Beijing. His petition was successful, and the ban was lifted in 1912 (Chou 1997: 139). Although all-female troupes had begun to emerge in public theatre towards the end of the nineteenth century, the peak of cultural fascination with the sexually ambiguous figure of the male *dan* occurred during the golden age of Beijing opera in the 1920s and 1930s, epitomised by the iconic Mei Lanfang (1894–1961). In the People's Republic of China, however, male cross-dressing is now on the verge of extinction, largely due to state policies that have phased out male *dan* training in Chinese opera schools. Meanwhile, female cross-dressing has managed to persist and even flourish in a relatively more supportive environment (Li 2003: 2). For further discussion, please refer to Chou, Hui-ling. 1997. "Striking Their Own Poses: The History of Cross-Dressing on the Chinese Stage." *The Drama Review* 41.2: 130-152; Li, Siu Leung. 2003. *Cross-Dressing in Chinese Opera Hong Kong*. Hong Kong University Press.

the Yuan Dynasty in the thirteenth century, often referred to by scholars as the "golden age" of Chinese theatre (Li 2003: 2). As Chou observes,

> In the Yuan period [1271–1368] a performer's sex was not the primary consideration for the role he or she played onstage. A character's gender was represented through dress and gesture. The external determinants of dress and gesture are the primary sites where a culture regulates gender differences in everyday life as well as on the stage. And because these external determinants could be put on and taken off, they were manipulated by artists onstage and were recognized by the society as art (Chou 1997: 134).

This concept of gender as performance holds the promise of transgressive potential, allowing an actress to step beyond her prescribed gender role. However, Chou highlights how this potential was undermined by the authorities' strict control over performers' conduct both onstage and offstage. Onstage, cross-dressing was tightly regulated. The combination of male and female elements in actresses' costumes underscored the performative nature of their disguises, reducing the shock of cross-gender performance and emphasizing the distinction between their onstage roles and everyday gender. This practice reinforced the separation between stage performance and real life, as well as the gender dichotomy. Offstage, the Yuan government's stringent regulations further constrained actresses. Isolated from the general public and classified as the lowest class in society, performers faced severely limited social mobility. Female performers, in particular, endured greater oppression than their male counterparts, often being treated like prostitutes for violating societal norms by appearing in public. These harsh restrictions not only degraded the social status of performers but also suppressed the transgressive power of cross-dressing onstage, neutralizing any potential social advantages (Chou 1997: 134–5).

Chou further explores the practice of cross-dressing beyond the Yuan Dynasty, examining its manifestations in both public and private spheres. According to her, true transgressive cross-dressing emerged in modern China at the beginning of the twentieth century, not on stage, but in real life with the rise of women revolutionaries as cross-dressers. At the turn of the century, elite women in China initiated the country's first feminist movement. Influenced by Western ideas, they established anti-foot-binding associations, girls' schools, and newspapers. The Republican Revolution, led by Sun Yat-sen (1866–1925), galvanized elite women to join male revolutionaries, forming radical groups like The Women's Military Troops of the Northern Expedition to oppose Manchurian rulers. These women often adopted male attire and behaviors, such as wearing men's clothing, using vulgar language, and engaging in public acts of defiance. A prominent figure in this movement was Qiu Jin (1875–1907), born into a gentry family and educated in *sishu* (private academy).⁷ She later moved to Japan, where she embraced modern revolutionary thought and radicalism, becoming known for her "flamboyant" conduct, including cross-dressing and practicing bomb-making and marksmanship (Rankin 1975: 52). Qiu Jin's actions symbolized a rebellion against Confucian norms, traditional marriages, and feminine roles, linking women's liberation with broader political causes. Her execution in 1907 made her an iconic figure of the New Woman during the Republican period (Chou 1997: 141).⁸

Chou's study of cross-dressing practices concludes with the May Fourth Movement (1919). However, the practice persisted through the Republic of China, the Sino-Japanese War, and culminated in Mao's socialist China from 1949 to the 1970s, extending into Tian's directing era from the 1990s to the twenty-first century. As Chou rightly argues, each instance of cross-dressing, whether onstage or offstage, carries distinct sociocultural and historical significance (Chou 1997: 131).

In this regard, Tian's gender presentation diverges from the transgressive practices of early twentieth-century revolutionary women. Her approach in the early twenty-first century is more practical and contained, reflecting the archetype of warrior women on the traditional stage, such as Hua Mulan, while also invoking the image of socialist idealized working women in real life.

1.3 Tian's Mulan-Like Scenario

Surveying the long tradition of women performing male roles in China – onstage and off – makes clear that Tian's practice is more complex, multifaceted, and distinctive. As noted at the outset of this section, her gender shifts both converse with and depart from the classical archetype of Hua Mulan.

---

⁷ In feudal China, a *sishu* (private academy), was a type of informal, privately-run educational institution, typically located in a scholar's home or a small building. These schools were a key feature of the educational system, especially in the imperial era, before modern schools and universities were established.a sishu offered instruction in classical Chinese literature, Confucian texts, and sometimes other subjects such as calligraphy and poetry. They were primarily attended by male students, with a focus on preparing young men for the imperial examination system, which was the primary path to official government positions.Sishu was usually run by a scholar or teacher, often a retired or former government official, who would impart knowledge and moral teachings to the students. The education was often rigorous, centred around memorisation and recitation of classical texts, and based on Confucian ideals of virtue, filial piety, and respect for tradition.

⁸ Qiu Jin was involved in various revolutionary activities, including plotting to assassinate government officials and join the efforts of the *Tongmenghui* (Revolutionary Alliance) that sought to overthrow the Qing dynasty. In 1907, Qiu Jin was arrested by the Qing authorities. After a quick trial, she was sentenced to death. On July 15, 1907, she was executed by beheading in the city of Hangzhou, at the age of 31. Her execution was a significant event in the revolutionary history of China and made her a martyr for the cause of women's rights and political change.

Crucially, Mulan functions not only as a figure in storytelling and performance but also as a category in feminist discourse. Dai Jinhua (1959–), one of China's leading feminist scholars, offers a widely cited reading of a "Mulan-like" scenario in which women are obliged to perform masculinity to meet expectations embedded in their social or professional roles (Dai 2007: 18).

Dai develops this concept while refuting Julia Kristeva's observations in her 1974 book *About Chinese Women*. In this book, Kristeva describes her journey from Paris through China's major cities and back during the late Cultural Revolution in 1974. Amidst the coincidental historical convergence of Western feminism and the Chinese Cultural Revolution, Kristeva offers a romantic and utopian portrayal of Chinese women. Her narrative spans from ancient times under the Confucian regime, through the revolution, and into the 1970s, attempting to capture the evolving roles and perceptions of women in Chinese society. She suggests that ancient Chinese women who emerged from silence to make their mark on the world could only achieve excellence "on the condition that she ceases to live as a woman." She illustrates this with the story of Mulan:

> One prototype that has served as a model for many Chinese girls and women who have wished to abandon a strictly feminine role and gain access to the political sphere is Hua Mulan, the heroine of the Five Dynasties (420–588). A legendary figure, she has remained famous because of an anonymous poet who sang her praises in the famous "Song of Mulan." So much does she love her father that, when he is called to battle against the Tartars and finds himself unable to go, she goes in his place, disguised as a man. For twelve years, Hua Mulan serves as a transvestite in the army, without anyone suspecting her. Once victory is won, she puts back on her make-up and her women's clothes: a quick-change act, a permanent masquerade (as a man and as a woman) that spares this Chinese Clorinda the tragedy of ours. This story repeats itself, in legend and reality, throughout the years of China's past; but we find it even today in the manuals of young Chinese describing the war against Japan (Kristeva 1977: 93).

The misunderstanding in Kristeva's interpretation lies in viewing Mulan as a rebellious figure or trickster who seamlessly transitions between her feminine status and male disguise. However, in the ballad, Mulan's journey – from leaving home to going to battle and then returning to her feminine role – is not an act of rebellion, but one of conformity. As Joseph R. Allen notes, the "Song of Mulan" is "not primarily a story of military action, but rather one of returning home" (Allen 1996: 346).

This conformity is further emphasized in one of the earliest plays about Mulan, *Ci Mulan tifu congjun* (Maid Mulan Joins the Army in Her Father's

Stead), written by Xu Wei (1521–1593) during the Ming Dynasty. In Xu's version, Mulan is honored by the emperor, returns home, sheds her male disguise, reunites with her family, and marries as arranged by her father. Furthermore, Xu Wei's play introduces a foot-binding motif absent from the original "Song of Mulan," written before foot-binding became prevalent. In the first act, Mulan unbinds her feet to disguise herself as a man before embarking on her military adventure, highlighting a dynamic of containment and subversion. The bound foot, a symbol of women's ultimate subjugation in late imperial China, is temporarily undone by Mulan to assume a male role, thereby challenging patriarchal constraints. While the play showcases Mulan's military prowess, it also depicts her concern about marriage prospects upon returning with enlarged feet. However, this anxiety is alleviated by a magical soaking treatment that re-shrinks her feet, reassuring spectators of her return to traditional femininity. This narrative translates all progressiveness and transformative potentiality into the traditional values of filiality (for the family) and loyalty (for the country) (Li 2003: 87).

In her book *Crossing the Ford: Contemporary Chinese Women's Writing and Feminine Culture*, Dai connects Mulan to the ancient Chinese tradition of women warriors known as Dao Madan. This role, often depicted in Peking Opera, is one that Tian herself trained in. According to Dai, throughout the male-dominated history of feudal China, women warriors gained historical visibility when they reluctantly took up arms to serve their kingdom, driven by filial duty to their fathers or loyalty to their husbands. Besides Mulan, this tradition is also depicted in the tales of "The Yang Family Generals," particularly in the popular Peking opera "Mu Guiying Takes Command." These narratives revolve around legendary heroines who, when all the men in their families have fallen in battle, and the nation faces grave threats from formidable enemies, have no choice but to step forward (Dai 2007:19).

Barbara M. Kaulbach, in her survey of historical records of military women and representations of the Chinese woman warrior in Chinese opera, argues that "[n]one of the woman warriors on the Chinese stage are allowed activities that could potentially bring about social change" (Kaulbach 1982: 77). She concludes that structurally these characters "behave in principally the same way: brave fighters in times of war, they resume their woman role at the end of the war" (Kaulbach 1982: 80).

Dai aligns with this argument and holds that, rather than carving out a new societal role, these female warriors operated within the patriarchal Confucian structure. Their actions are dictated by loyalty to the patriarchal figures of father and husband. A woman's rare rise to historical prominence and her dedication to the kingdom were fundamentally motivated by Confucian values (Dai

2007:19). This explains why Mulan's transvestism is not only excused but celebrated. In this context, Dai views the story of Mulan as a metaphor that reflects negatively on the situation of women in ancient China. She then extends the metaphorical critique to modern China in response to Kriteva's appreciation of the liberation of modern Chinese women after the revolution.

Kristeva's admiration of Mulan's story shows her investment in the idea of women identifying with men. She affirms the positive gains of the Chinese Revolution, in general, and the social policies of socialist China, in particular. She assumes that socialism, as a social order, is superior to capitalism and that both men and women benefit when liberated from feudal and class oppression. To her mind, the Chinese woman was no longer the signifier of a corrupt and backward society, as she threw off the shackles of her feudal past. Instead, she came to represent a utopian possibility for Western women – an alternative mode of femininity (Kristeva 1977: 198).

Kristeva's view of the special historical path of women's liberation in China is partly true. As in many colonized or semi-colonized societies, women's liberation began as an important part of national liberation (from feudalism and imperialism) and revolution led by the leftist Marxists in the 1920s. Moreover, it was reinforced by the Chinese Communist Party (CCP), which took power in the 1940s. Under the leadership of the CCP, the new China enacted several transformative laws, including the abolition of arranged marriages, the closure of brothels, and the eradication of prostitution, which collectively encouraged women to enter the workforce. Additionally, laws and regulations were passed to ensure women had equal rights and opportunities in employment and inheritance. These reforms marked a significant transition for Chinese women, moving them from domestic roles into broader societal participation, thereby unlocking their potential to contribute to social production. Through their work, many women found integration into society, making "work" a keyword and a reflection of women's fine qualities at that time. The image of a "working woman" became not only the socialist ideal but was also widely celebrated in literature (Yang and Yoon 2023: 694).

From the 1950s through the 1980s, the dominant popular narrative of gender was encapsulated in the line "Who said that women cannot be equal to men?" Originating in the 1950s from Chang Xiangyu's stage performances of the Yu opera *Hua Mulan*, and disseminated nationwide by the 1956 opera film, the line became a household catchphrase, resonating with official egalitarian rhetoric. It seems to echo what Kristeva notes – not without envy – Chinese women, "their lives now revolutionised," had become "so similar to the men" (Kristeva 1977: 198).

Dai Jinhua, however, voices a caution. The proudly "man-like" working woman risks eclipsing women's own concerns – for instance, how to find a foothold between the socialist glorification of laboring womanhood and the continuing pressures of traditional family ideology. In Dai's view, collectivist ideology promoted a unisex female ideal whose purpose was national service rather than self-realization. The line "Who says women are inferior to men?" implicitly installs men as the norm to which women must aspire, thereby reaffirming male dominance and eroding female subjectivity (Dai 2015). She writes,

> Between the old image of women as sufferers, victims, and shamed individuals and the new image of women as quasi-male warriors, the liberated, new women become lost in a historical void ... For modern Chinese women, "Mulan," a woman who disguises herself as a man and becomes a hero under a male identity, becomes the most important, if not the only, representation of women in mainstream ideology (Dai 2007:17–8).[9]

Given that Tian was born in the late 1960s and grew up within the framework of Maoist gender ideology that emphasized the "working woman" with a masculine image, her choice to adopt a masculine appearance as a theatre director parallels Dai's concept of the modern Mulan-like scenario. Tian shaped her manners and appearance to conform to a male template, meeting the social expectations of her role. When a woman seeks to enter this male-dominated and male-serving discursive system, she adopts the tone, concepts, and symbolic norms of men, thereby entering into discourse as a male homologue (Barlow 2004: 315). As Tian said, "I have always worked hard under the rules set by the physically stronger gender, striving to be just like them, requiring the same sense of space and strength" (qtd. in Zhou and Huang 2013). This masculine presentation offers her practical advantages in her profession but also perpetuates the notion that men are the preferred sex and that women should emulate men. Therefore, Tian's adoption of a Mulan-like persona does not challenge the conventional order but rather reinforces it. Tian's performance of masculinity is linked to Maoist gender politics, where women were encouraged to participate in social labor and pursue career advancement, but at the expense of their feminine bodies and identities (see Figure 2).

1.4 Tian's Strategy of Gender Performance

In June 2017, while directing the reproduction of *Hurricane*, Tian Qinxin suffered an acute attack of pancreatitis, an ordeal that brought her face-to-face

---

[9] Since the 1990s, as a backlash against the socialist women's movement, gender differences have been increasingly celebrated in contemporary Chinese society (Chen 2009: 57). However, the 1990s also marked the onset of regressive trends in post-socialist gender politics that persist today, as examined by various scholars. This period is characterized by a resurgence of traditional patriarchal values intertwined with global neoliberalism and consumerism. Within this context, women are primarily seen as consumers within a commercialized, state-defined domestic sphere.

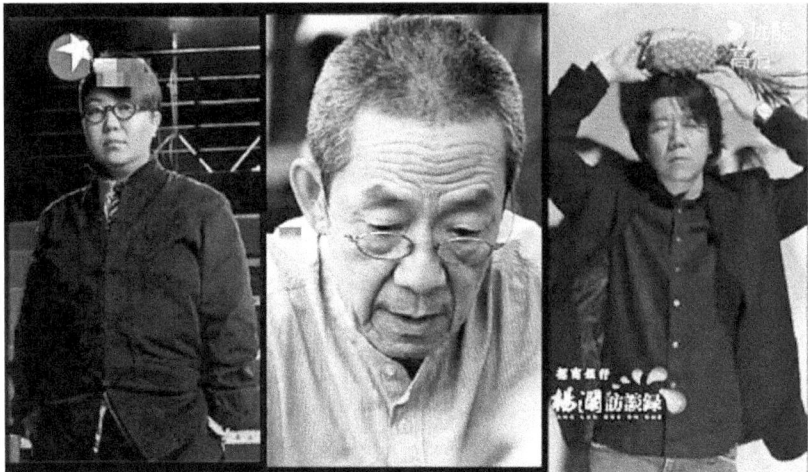

Figure 2 Tian Qinxin (left) featured alongside Lin Zhaohua and Meng Jinghui as one of the top three contemporary theatre directors in China, in Yang Lan One on One in 2012. Screenshot by the author from the interview "Tian Qinxin," *Yang Lan One on One*, hosted by Yang Lan, *Youku*, https://vo.youku.com/v_show/id_XNDU4MzY5MzIw.html. Accessed October 15, 2025.

with life-threatening circumstances. Following this, her image underwent a notable shift toward greater femininity. In an interview on Phoenix Television's weekly interview program *Mingren Mianduimian* (*Celebrity Face to Face,* often branded *SFace*) in 2022, she reflected on this transformation, explaining that, before her illness, she had adopted a more masculine appearance due to the stereotypical nature of a director's work. However, after being discharged from the hospital, her feminine side began to resurface. One of the first things she did upon leaving the hospital was to have her hair permed. She also shared that, although she had previously been indifferent to pearls, she suddenly found herself captivated by them while shopping and, unable to resist their allure, had bought a string of them for the very first time. This, of course, is Tian's own interpretation of her change. Interestingly, the same year she embraced this more feminine image also marked her ascension to the leadership of the NTC and her appointment as a female cadre in the CPPCC. In the interview, Tian casually remarked that it would have seemed rather odd for her to assume the role of theatre company leader while still presenting a masculine appearance (Tian and Tian 2022).

One can observe that Tian reverted to a feminine image to better suit her new role, since it is necessary for her to demonstrate her identity as both a female leader and a female president. This shift partly reflects a tacit rule within CCP leadership: Meeting criteria such as being a woman, belonging to a minority ethnic group, and being a non-Communist Party member increases the likelihood of promotion (a policy akin to affirmative action in the West). Tian's identity as a woman, a Manchurian, and a member of the China Democratic League checks all these boxes.[10]

However, women promoted under such criteria often hold symbolic positions with limited genuine power. Despite improvements in women's sociopolitical status during Mao's era, evidence indicates that Chinese women have seldom been central to power structures. This is reflected in their consistent underrepresentation in both the CCP and the Chinese government, and the rarity of female politicians reaching the most powerful positions in the political sphere (Howell 2014). Within local government, where the CCP has established quotas to promote women's political inclusion, female officials are frequently assigned roles associated with birth control, environmental sanitation, or medical insurance, rather than positions focused on economic development or infrastructure construction (Song 2016: 90). This division of responsibilities reflects the prevailing belief that such tasks are inherently "feminine" and, as such, more suitable for women. Similarly, Tian's role as president of the NTC is categorized as "feminine" due to its association with the cultural industry.

In this new role, Tian began to stage a feminized public persona consistent with mainstream expectations for a female leader. Her image now frequently features shoulder-length hair, a Chinese *qipao* (Cheongsam) dress, and a pearl necklace. In a pattern reminiscent of the legendary Mulan, her trajectory is one of cyclical gendering – moving from femininity to masculinity and back again. In this sense, her gender presentation has at times aligned with dominant ideological expectations: first, a masculinized director's habitus of authority; later, a feminized leadership style signaling incorporation into the cultural establishment. Yet alongside such conformity, Tian mobilizes cross-gender performance strategically – and with agency – in deciding when and how to adopt or discard such a persona. That agency is shaped both by the socioeconomic conditions of her era and by her own personal poetics (see Figure 3).

Tian's rise to prominence coincides with the revitalization and commercialization of theatre in China since the 1990s. She has been embraced and nurtured by her institution, and from her debut production onward, each of her works has

---

[10] The China Democratic League (CDL), abbreviated as Minmeng, is a component of the patriotic united front led by the CCP and is one of the current democratic parties in the People's Republic of China. As a participating party that collaborates closely with the CCP, it mainly consists of high and intermediate-level intellectuals engaged in culture, education, and scientific and technological work. The CDL possesses characteristics of a political alliance and is committed to the cause of building socialism with Chinese characteristics.

Figure 3 Tian Qinxin as President of the NTC in the interview "*Tian Qinxin: On the Centenary of the Communist Party of China, Discussing the Responsibility of the National Theatre of China*" in 2021. Screenshot by the author from the interview video, *Haokan*, https://haokan.baidu.com/v?pd=wisenatural& vid=8229384843565243535. Accessed October 15, 2025.

garnered significant attention and support. On most occasions, Tian has had the freedom to stage her chosen productions, utilizing the finest resources available in Chinese theatre, and collaborating with some of the most prominent actors in the field. Her directorial vision has been fully supported, and she has enjoyed a large amount of autonomy in directing her projects.

Two influential male figures within the system have been pivotal to her career development: one as a leader and the other as a marketer. The first of these is Zhao Youliang (1944–2023), then-President of the Beijing-based Central Experimental Theatre (CET). Upon witnessing her debut play, *Breaking Wrist*, Zhao immediately offered her a place in his institution, stating that there was a need for female directors (Zhou and Huang 2013). He subsequently provided unwavering support for Tian's production of *The Field of Life and Death*. Tian herself has acknowledged that, without Zhao's backing, the play would never have come to fruition (Tian 2003: 221). In 1999, at the age of 30, Tian adapted and directed Xiao Hong's novel *The Field of Life and Death*, a production that went on to sweep major theatre awards, including the Cao Yu Drama Literature Award, the Ministry of Culture's Cultural Prize, and the Director's Prize.

Tian's adaptation of *The Field of Life and Death* attracted significant attention, even though Tian encountered questions from journalists that, at times, bordered on the sexist – such as the question of how, as a woman, she could possess such a strong sense of national identity. Despite this, the play received widespread acclaim from both the public and the academic community, even becoming a literary event in its own right. Scholars have remarked that it was the play with the most profound impact on both academia and society in 1999 (Wang et al. 2010: 32). The prestigious intellectual journal *Du Shu* (Reading) hosted a symposium on Tian's adaptation, inviting leading scholars such as Qian Liqun, Li Tuo, and Wang Hui to discuss it. The Chinese Writers' Association also organized a special viewing, inviting fifty writers from Beijing, including Liang Xiaosheng and Bi Shumin. Moreover, the cast of Beijing People's Art Theatre's production of *Teahouse*, led by director Lin Zhaohua, attended a performance as well. Such recognition and professional advancement are unusual for a woman of thirty, especially within the context of contemporary Chinese theatre.

Another important figure in Tian's career is Li Dong, a producer with whom she has collaborated for over two decades, beginning with *The Field of Life and Death*. Li joined CET in 1991 but spent the next seven years working in advertising, which prepared him to apply his expertise when the theatre adopted a market-oriented management approach in 1998 (Chou 2016: 167). In 1999, another prominent theatre director, Meng Jinghui, began working on his commercial hit *Rhino in Love* and exploring the market. That same year, the newly established National Theatre introduced a producer-driven model, and Li Dong and Tian were paired together as a result. Reflecting on their first collaboration, Li recalls that his role was primarily to manage crises. He observed that few were interested in a play with the words "life" and "death" in its title. Instead of opting for conventional advertising aimed at the general public, Li's marketing campaign targeted cultural elites. He did promotions through internal publications of the Ministry of Culture and official government newspapers (Ma 2010). When the play faced significant criticism from theatre experts – some even calling for its closure – Li responded by inviting key cultural figures to attend the performances. He was also the one who organized the forum, hosted by *Du Shu*, which helped to calm the negative press (Wang 2011).

As Katherine Hui-Ling Chou observes, Li excelled not only in navigating political policies but also in marketing to the rapidly emerging urban middle class in China (Chou 2016: 165–6). Following the commercialization of Chinese theatre in 2000, Li dedicated himself to the promotion and marketing of each of Tian's productions. Tian has expressed a sentiment similar to her remarks about Zhao Youliang: "Without Li Dong, there would be no theatre for us" (Wang 2011). The partnership between Tian and Li was widely celebrated by the media and the NTC, particularly for their highly successful 2010 stage adaptation of *The Yellow Storm*. The production was hailed as a model for the industrial potential of Chinese huaju theatre, and Tian was ranked among the top ten highest-grossing huaju directors in the first decade of the twenty-first century (Chou 2016: 162). Li Dong's most significant contribution lies in his steadfast protection of Tian's artistic freedom and independence, enabling her to navigate the complex landscape of institutional, administrative, and commercial pressures with greater autonomy.

To sum up, Tian's success is deeply intertwined with the rapid socioeconomic transformations China underwent in the late 1990s, a period marked by an insatiable hunger for talent. During this time, industries across the country were expanding, and individuals with exceptional abilities were highly valued and actively sought after. Tian recalls the period between her adaptations of *The Field of Life and Death* (1999) and *The Orphan of Zhao* (2003), describing it as an era brimming with opportunities. For those with keen instincts to identify and seize them, success became almost inevitable (Ma 2010). Moreover, Tian's fortunate encounter with Zhao Youliang and Li Dong – two male colleagues who have provided consistent and unwavering support – has been crucial to her career. In this light, her gender identity is characterized by a dual quality: a strategic conformity that allows her to assume different roles with ease at various stages of her career, and a playful flexibility that enables her to effortlessly navigate and juggle these roles with confidence and creativity.

The ease and playfulness of Tian's gender performance are also rooted in a personal poetics shaped by her deep knowledge of Chinese performing arts. As she repeatedly underscores in interviews, her approach to appearance draws from the principles of Chinese *xi* (music theatre, opera), where actors commonly *zhuanglong banhu* (pretend to be dragons and tigers) and *tiaojin tiaochu* (jump in and out of roles) (Yang 2012). This method resembles Bertolt Brecht's strategy of alienation, in which actors, shifting between roles, are compelled to engage with characters through rational and dialectical thinking. Yet, in Chinese traditional performance, the transformation between roles is marked by ease and delight, aiming to balance the illusory and the real, the serious and the comic. The goal is to foster a relaxed, joyous interaction between the performer and the audience (Zhang 2024).

In *The Novel and Theatrical Imagination in Early Modern China*, Mei Chun highlights that a core feature of *xi* is "playacting, masquerades, metamorphoses," citing definitions of *xi* in the *Kangxi Zidian* (the Kangxi Dictionary), *Ciyuan* (Lexicology), and *Cihai* (Sea of Words), which describe it as involving *xinong* (playing tricks) or *xishua* (playing around) (Mei 2011: 14). The celebration of playfulness has long been integral to traditional Chinese theatre. While many modern scholars trace the origins of Chinese theatre to ritual, the Song dynasty polymath Su Shi (1037–1101) viewed *xi* as a social distribution of pleasurable energy, distinguishing it from ritual practices. For Su Shi, the essence of *xi* lies in playacting and impersonation, free from moral constraints. Playwrights have often described the allure of *xi* as offering them the freedom to assign roles and engage in role-playing, thus breaking free from social fixities (Mei 2011: 16–7). Mei coins "playful theatricals" as the dominant mode for celebrating the fluidity of identities, roles, and persons, while implicitly and explicitly questioning moral and orthodox fixities (Mei 2011: 221).

The concept of "playful theatricals" can also be applied to Tian's gender presentation. Her approach reveals a playful and light-hearted quality made possible by the support she has received and a favorable period in Chinese theatre. Indeed, Tian's adaptive and playful approach to assuming different gendered roles in her own life parallels her directorial vision, in which role-playing frequently becomes a central artistic strategy.

The final decade of the twentieth century marked a period of intensified economic reforms and the subsequent restructuring of China's theatre system. This created the conditions for the emergence of three dominant categories of theatre from the early 2000s onward: main melody, experimental, and commercial. These categories, however, were not mutually exclusive. Artists consistently sought to redefine their aesthetic expressions, striving to maximize their creative potential, personal freedom, and financial stability. With significant institutional support, Tian has excelled at playing this game. The following two sections will explore her adaptations within this context.

2 Adapting Works by Chinese Women Novelists

This section will examine Tian Qinxin's adaptations of significant works by modern Chinese women novelists, including Xiao Hong's *The Field of Life and Death* (1999), Eileen Chang's *Red Rose, White Rose* (2007), and Lilian Lee Pik-Wah's *Green Snake* (2013). In *A Theory of Adaptation*, Linda Hutcheon identifies four key motivations for adapters: economic incentives, legal constraints, cultural capital, and personal and political motives (Hutcheon 2006: 86–95). All of these factors are pertinent in analyzing Tian's adaptations. Hutcheon also argues that adaptation is invariably contextual – embedded in a particular historical moment and cultural milieu rather than existing in isolation. Given that tastes and values are context-dependent, many adapters modernize the temporal setting to generate present-day resonance (Hutcheon 2006: 142). Tian's adaptations of these three works by women writers similarly reflect the sociohistorical conditions of her time. Tian's adaptation of *The Field of Life and Death* exhibited a pronounced feminist sensibility and a strong nationalist agenda. Set in rural Northeast China during the 1920s and 1930s, the play poignantly underscores women's suffering under patriarchal oppression and the Japanese invasion. However, this early work contrasts with her later, twenty-first-century adaptations, created at a time when state policy meant that, as a director, Tian faced pressure to boost box office sales. In consequence, as the following analysis demonstrates, Tian had to balance gender awareness and artistic ambition with market demands. Ultimately, this explains why her adaptations of Eileen Chang and Lilian Lee Pik-Wah's works, with a focus on themes of romantic love and sexuality, appealed to the tastes of urban middle-class audiences. Featuring all-star casts and spectacular stage productions, these adaptations achieved significant box office success.[11]

In addition to discussing sentiment and feminist sensibility, this section will identify and explain Tian's adaptation strategies and her distinctive style, characterized by hybridity and syncretism. This includes her blending of traditional Chinese opera elements – such as stylized gestures and choreography – with modern spoken drama, as well as the integration of Chinese theatrical traditions with Western forms, like Antonin Artaud's Theatre of Cruelty and Pina Bausch's dance theatre. Tian's style is also distinguished by the "playful theatricals" discussed in the previous section, which draw inspiration from Chinese traditional performing arts. These playful theatricals – embodied in practices such as *Tiaoji tiaochu* (jumping in and out of roles) and self-reflexivity – are evident not only in the expression of her own gender identity but also as a strategic element in her adaptations. Even in her first adaptation of *The Field of Life and Death*, which addresses profound and weighty themes, Tian structured the play with a playful, almost childlike approach, akin to assembling and dismantling Lego blocks. This sense of playfulness becomes even more prominent in her postmodern adaptations of *Red Rose, White Rose,* and *Green Snake*. In these works, Tian oscillates between the serious and the playful, conveying her messages with depth while also entertaining her audience.

In her adaptation of *The Field of Life and Death*, Tian transformed Xiao Hong's prose-like novel into a workable stage script by restructuring its fragmented narrative and integrating feminist and nationalist themes, even though these remain in tension in the original text. By employing stylized movement,

---

[11] Tian's stage adaptations often sold out, demonstrating her ability to attract audiences. In 2013, Tian's success was evident with a total box office of 54.26 million RMB from three major plays in 2012, surpassing renowned directors like Meng Jinghui and Lai Shengchuan in earnings. This achievement solidified her status as a leading figure in mainstream Chinese theatre. See "The first domestic annual box office ranking for performing arts is released" 2013. People.cn. http://culture.people.com.cn/n/2013/0524/c172318-21600665.html, accessed on May 17, 2024.

sculptural tableaux, and minimalist lighting, she created a powerful theatrical effect that sharply contrasted with the realist conventions dominant in contemporary spoken drama.

Unlike her adaptation of *The Field of Life and Death*, which Tian undertook out of personal passion and empathy for Xiao Hong, her staging of Eileen Chang's *Red Rose, White Rose* was shaped more by the commercial imperatives of the twenty-first-century Chinese theatre industry and state policies promoting theatre as part of the cultural sector. The production employed bold devices – a central glass corridor symbolizing desire, double-cast "split selves," and the spatial contrast between the two "roses" – to dramatize the dichotomies at the heart of Chang's novella. While these innovations added theatrical energy and ensured commercial appeal, critics observed that they undercut the tragic irony and desolate undertones of the original, reducing the subtle complexity of Chang's work.

Tian's 2013 *Green Snake* pushes female sexuality to the fore by charting Little Green's sexual awakening and insistence on the freedom to love, set against Madame White's Confucian ideal of wife-and-motherhood. Imbued with her signature playfulness and meta-theatrical style, the production allowed characters to step in and out of the narrative, inviting both reflection and laughter. At the same time, Tian integrated stylized gestures from Chinese opera, using actors trained in Peking opera to embody serpentine sensuality through delicate strides, entwining motions, and symbolic gestures of desire. This fusion of feminist emphasis, playful theatricality, and operatic movement produced a bold reimagining of the legend that underscored Tian's distinctive aesthetic.

2.1 Adapting Xiao Hong's *The Field of Life and Death* (1999): The Female Body and National Consciousness

The *Field of Life and Death*, which premiered at the China National Children's Theatre in Beijing in 1999, marked Tian Qinxin's first significant adaptation. This play holds a special place in the evolution of contemporary Chinese theatre at the turn of the twenty-first century, generating extensive discussion among drama and literary circles, as well as captivating general audiences. It has been canonized, winning numerous major awards and becoming a cornerstone of the NTC's repertoire. It was revived twice: in 2004, to commemorate the sixtieth anniversary of the victory in the War of Resistance against Japan, and again in 2015, to celebrate the seventieth anniversary. Despite its later canonization and politicization by the NTC and academia, Tian's adaptation of *The Field of Life and Death* originated from her deep love for Xiao Hong. Tian has often stated that she began reading Xiao Hong's work as a teenager and has been captivated ever since (Tian 2003: 214). Therefore, when Tian chose the play for her first major production at the NTC in 1999, the choice reflected both her artistic temperament and her self-identification with Xiao Hong.

On June 2, 1911, Xiao Hong was born into a declining landlord family in Heilongjiang Province, Northeast China. In 1931, at the age of 20, she fled with her boyfriend to escape an arranged marriage, embarking on a turbulent life as a writer scarred by poverty and exile. Her struggles were compounded by the challenges of being a woman in a feudal society and the hardships brought by the Japanese invasion. Tragically, she met an untimely death in Hong Kong in 1942 at a young age. Xiao Hong wrote her first novel, *The Field of Life and Death,* at the age of 24. Set in the rural outskirts of Harbin around the time of the 1931 Mukden Incident (an event marking the beginning of the Japanese invasion of Manchuria),[12] the novel offers a grim and powerful depiction of peasant life in Northeast China. The novel does not adhere to a conventional plot structure. Instead, it weaves together various vignettes that collectively depict the villagers' experiences, illustrating how poverty, ignorance, class oppression, and patriarchy reduce rural people, especially women, to an almost animalistic existence. It is only under the threat of the Japanese invasion that they awaken to their humanity, gaining a sense of subjectivity and agency. As its English translator Howard Goldblatt comments, it evoked strong emotions of anger, pity, and outrage in its contemporary readers – outrage not only against the external forces that demeaned and brutalized the villagers but also against the peasants' own fatalistic, passive, and conservative mentality (Goldblatt 2002: xiii). For Tian, this visceral intensity was precisely what compelled her to take on the play: She later remarked that she felt a natural kinship with Xiao Hong, describing her as talented, young, and naïve – a kindred spirit who persisted despite adversity (Tian 2019). In her production, Tian drew upon both the nationalist legacy of the novel and the gender tensions that Xiao Hong foregrounded. In doing so, she participates in the debates over Xiao Hong's positioning in Chinese modern literature.

There is no doubt that Xiao Hong occupies a canonical place in modern Chinese literature. Lu Xun (1881–1936), widely regarded as the greatest modern Chinese writer and a leading figure in Chinese literature, mentored and supported Xiao Hong during her times of dire need. He assisted in the publication of this novel and wrote a highly laudatory preface for it. He later remarked

---

[12] On September 18, 1931, a minor anti-Japanese incident occurred near the southern Manchurian city of Mukden (now Shenyang). The ensuing Japanese retaliation led to the formalization of Japanese control over all of Manchuria and the establishment of the puppet regime of Manchukuo in early 1932.

to American journalist Edgar Snow that Xiao Hong was among the finest leftist writers in China (Liu 1995: 201). As Lydia H. Liu acutely points out, this is partly due to Lu Xun's laudatory comments and "also because, in the eyes of the majority of male critics, she did not confine herself to the 'triviality of women's lives but reached out to broader themes of national survival and anti-imperialist struggle" (Liu 1995: 199). Indeed, *The Field of Life and Death* has long been heralded as one of the two most important early examples of anti-Japanese literature. The other one, *Village in August*, was written by one of Xiao Hong's lovers, Xiao Jun (Goldblatt 2002: xiii). Consequently, interpretations of *The Field of Life and Death* often center on concepts of national character and national allegory, initially framed by both Lu Xun and Hu Feng. Hu Feng (1902–1985), a prominent literary critic and writer, praised the anti-Japanese spirit of the book and the awakening of the Chinese peasantry to nationalism: "These ant-like, ignorant men and women, sad but resolute, stood on the front line of the sacred war of nationalism. Once they were like ants, living in order to die. Now they were titans, dying in order to live" (qtd in Liu 1995: 201).

Tian echoes Hu Feng's glorification of the villagers in the climactic final act of her adaptation, with a heightened, almost hysterical intensity. Led by a grief-stricken older woman mourning her daughter killed by Japanese soldiers, the villagers surge toward the enemy in a frenzy of slogans and defiance:

Wang Po (overcome with grief): The way of dying is no longer the same!
[Drums thunder]
[Man 1 slowly rises. Then Man 2, Man 3 ... one after another, the villagers stand]

Cheng Ye: Brothers, young and old! Strike – down – the devils!
[He hurls himself at the Japanese soldiers. Gunfire cracks, but the crowd, fearless before the violence, surges forward and clashes with the enemy.]

Zhao San: ... When I'm laid in my grave, you must plant the flag of China at its peak. I am Chinese! I want the Chinese flag ... I will not be a slave to a conquered nation.

Cheng Ye: Brothers! Do you know what day it is today? Today, we go to meet death without fear! Even if our heads hang from every treetop in the village, we will go willingly. Is that not so!?

All: Yes! Even if we are hacked to pieces, we go willingly! (Tian 2010b: 290)

However, from a gender politics perspective, Liu questions this male-dominated and nation-oriented narrative, arguing that it erases the tensions in Xiao Hong's exploration of the relationship between women and nationhood

(Liu 1995: 200). For Liu, the fields of *sheng* (birth, life) and *si* (death) primarily represent the experiences of the female body, which are often linked to bleeding, injury, deformation, or death from childbirth, physical abuse, sickness, suicide, or slaughter (Liu 1995: 201). Given that the female body already suffers greatly under patriarchal oppression, there is an inherent incompatibility between collective nationalist consciousness and individual female subjectivity, especially against the backdrop of foreign invasion. As Liu notes, "the omnipresence of the female body casts an ominous shadow over nationalist discourse" (Liu 1995: 203). Liu further emphasizes that,

> Xiao Hong deals primarily with the life of women whose oppression makes it difficult to idealize the patriarchal society before or after the Japanese occupation. Whatever happens to the nation, the female body always suffers the most. The final chapters of her novel make it clear that national identity is largely a male prerogative; it allows the village men to acquire national consciousness and preach the new gospel to their women despite their own lowly status in society (Liu 1995: 208).

This raises a set of questions: If nationalism bestows a new sense of heroic identity upon male villagers, what does it offer women? How does Xiao Hong reconcile her feminist sensibility with the grand national narrative? Meng Yue and Dai Jinhua observe in *Fuchu lishi dibiao* (Emerging from the horizon of history) that shortly after the outbreak of the War of Resistance against Japan, Xiao Hong encountered multiple crises involving national identity, romantic relationships, and her role as a woman. She was compelled to choose between aligning with the dominant anti-Japanese cultural paradigm or asserting her feminine self. The former option, though widely anticipated and offering safety and stability, required compliance. In contrast, the latter choice entailed solitary struggle, risk, and uncertainty. According to Meng and Dai, Xiao Hong chose the latter path. Instead of following the tide of intellectuals and artists heading to Yan'an, a major revolutionary base known for its anti-Japanese resistance efforts and cultural significance during the Chinese Communist movement, Xiao Hong went into exile in Hong Kong, where she fell ill and died tragically young at the age of thirty-one (Meng and Dai 2018: 203–4).

Just as she chose the less trodden path in life, Xiao Hong presents the tension between the collective (or rather male-dominated) nationalist discourse and female experiences in *The Field of Life and Death* without attempting to reconcile it. So, how did Tian handle this tension from the 1930s when adapting the work at the end of the 1990s, a time of resurging nationalist sentiment? Tian's production coincided with the tragic American bombing of the Chinese Embassy in Belgrade on May 7, 1999, during the NATO bombing campaign in the Kosovo War. The incident provoked a surge of nationalist sentiment in China, manifesting itself in widespread protests, as many saw it as a direct affront to China's sovereignty.

It took Tian two years to adapt Xiao Hong's prose-like novel into a workable play script, which she shaped into a prologue and six acts with a tighter plot and more defined characterization. As noted earlier, Tian echoes the views of critics who praised Xiao's treatment of nationalism, emphasizing how the originally ignorant and passive villagers are awakened by the Japanese invasion, so that deaths once likened to those of animals are transformed into the heroic sacrifices of national martyrs. One of the central characters, Cheng Ye, who eventually leads the villagers in resisting the Japanese, is initially portrayed as selfish and driven by animal-like sexual impulses. He is attracted to a young village girl, Golden Bough, and forces himself on her, resulting in her pregnancy. His father, Two-and-a-Half Li, a broken-spirited and submissive man, believes that hosting Japanese soldiers would earn him respect from the villagers. However, despite his hospitality, the soldiers rape and kill his wife. It is only after Japanese troops raid the village and Golden Bough is murdered that Cheng finally succeeds in rallying the people to fight, with even his weak and submissive father, Two-and-a-Half Li, taking up arms.

Focusing on the theme of life and death, the play's narrative connects moments of life (pregnancy, childbirth, resurrection) and death (homicide, suicide, death by Japanese brutality), highlighting the villagers' ignorance and apathy until they are finally awakened by the Japanese invasion. Tian mentioned that she perceived a touch of childlike candor and mischief in twenty-four-year-old Xiao Hong, aligning well with her temperament and her concept of theatre as a form of play (Tian 2003: 215). There is a sense of naivety and cruelty in manipulating the fates of these villagers in the novel, and she decided to pursue this further on stage. Her adaptation employs significant contrasts and deliberate acts of destruction. The concept of playful destruction is akin to a child playing with a collage game: Adults painstakingly assemble it, and the child quickly dismantles it, finding joy in the process. For instance, in the scene where a peasant kills a thief, everyone believes he has killed the landlord. The villagers shift from fear to joy, imagining a bright future. Suddenly, the landlord appears, shattering their hopes. Similarly, after Two-and-a-Half Li's attempt to arrange a marriage between his son Cheng Ye and Golden Bough through her father, Zhao San, is rejected, he hosts Japanese soldiers in his home, believing they will support him. Just as the audience starts to relax, the rape incident occurs, leading to the death of Two-and-a-Half Li's wife, once again shattering expectations (Tian 2003: 215).

Although Tian stated that she did not have any specific "isms" in mind during the adaptation process, the stage play exhibits strong feminist and nationalist themes. The play opens with a prologue featuring a woman giving birth, symbolizing her body as a field of life and death: The stage is enveloped in darkness. A single overhead light illuminates three men and one woman. In this stark light, the woman's inverted body position is highlighted, with her legs splayed open toward the sky. Her pale legs and red shoes stand out sharply against the darkness. This statue-like image of the female body giving birth seems to set a tone that aligns with Liu's feminist reading. Throughout the novel, women give birth easily and excessively, yet this fertility is portrayed negatively. The newborn babies often face poverty, sickness, and violence, and the painful act of childbirth inflicts severe punishment on the female body, as Xiao Hong vividly describes in chapter six of her novel, entitled "Days of Punishment" (Xiao 2002: 43) (see Figure 4).

However, aside from the visually striking prologue, the theme of the female body as a field of life and death is not as thoroughly explored in the play as in the original novel. The plot of the play primarily focuses on class conflict between peasants and landlords, and the ensuing national crisis caused by the Japanese invasion. Tian attempts to organize the plot and build all the events toward the villagers' resistance against the Japanese. The most symbolic events are the rapes of two village women: Two-and-a-Half Li's wife in Act Two and Golden

Figure 4 Giving-birth scene from *The Field of Life and Death*. Screenshot by the author from the recorded performance, *The Field of Life and Death*, *Bilibili*, www.bilibili.com/video/BV14Z8eziETx/?p=84. Accessed October 15, 2025.

Bough in Act Six, the latter of which directly triggers the resistance. As Liu observes, rape, with its usual associations with female sexuality and femininity, becomes one of the most commonly used tropes in national literature and anti-imperialist propaganda (Liu 1995: 197). Tian's utilization of the trope marks a clear departure from the original novel, where the most humiliating rape inflicted on Golden Bough is committed by a Chinese man, not a Japanese soldier. Consequently, unlike the male peasants, the peasant woman Golden Bough never succeeds in becoming a national subject, as the physical experiences forced upon her by her husband and the rapist contradict the national identity imposed by the presence of the Japanese (Liu 1995: 199).

In addition, Goldblatt observes that Xiao Hong avoids presenting an idealized, patriotic-romantic perspective of the war of resistance. Instead, she focuses on the isolated and personal effects it has on individuals in everyday situations. Rather than depicting the war within a broad historical context, Xiao Hong subtly yet forcefully illuminates the individual tragedies experienced by people who, like herself, are brutalized by incomprehensible violence (Goldblatt, xv). In contrast, Tian's adaptation crystallizes this fragmented and clouded comprehension of war suddenly and dramatically. In the final act of the play, villagers who moments earlier had no concept of national identity undergo an abrupt transformation into national subjects, fervently shouting slogans such as, "A person with dignity does not become a slave to a fallen nation!" "Today, we go to save our country!" and "I am Chinese!" This climactic shift aligns with the nationalist trend of the 1990s and contributes significantly to the classification of the play as "main melody theatre" (Liu 2016: 325). In Hong Kong, it was perceived as resembling *yangbanxi* (model dramas) (Tian 2010a: 61). Both labels are not particularly complimentary, as main melody plays are produced by state-owned companies to win government awards crucial for the theatres' financial survival, while model dramas are seen as a legacy of the Cultural Revolution, intended for political propaganda (Mackerras 2008: 5).

Despite these labels, the play garnered significant acclaim for its stagecraft and theatrical approaches that diverged from the conventional spoken theatre. *Huaju* (spoken theatre) began in the first decade of the twentieth century, drawing inspiration from the Western Ibsenesque tradition. It was promoted as a potent alternative to traditional operatic theatre, which incorporated singing, dancing, and acrobatics (Chen 2002: 25). Siyuan Liu summarises its evolution, noting its hybrid beginnings that blended indigenous and Western theatre, a long period of commitment to realism in mid century, a rediscovery of indigenous performance combined with avant-garde experimentation since the late 1970s (Liu 2016: 311). According to Liu, *huaju*'s formal experimentation began in the late 1970s, driven by the excitement of rediscovering world theatre in the twentieth century after three decades of fossilized knowledge that had remained fixed on Ibsen and Stanislavski. Translations of modern theatre – including symbolism, expressionism, Bertolt Brecht, and the Theatre of the Absurd – became the center of vibrant intellectual discourse (Liu 2016: 315). Theatre practitioners also discovered that certain conventions of traditional Chinese theatre resonated with Western modern theatre approaches, realizing that these elements could enhance contemporary plays (Mackerras 2008: 10).

Tian was among these innovative practitioners. She acknowledged the significant influence of French director Antonin Artaud (1896–1948), the founder of the Theatre of Cruelty, and Pina Bausch (1940–2009), the German pioneer of Dance Theatre (Tian et al. 2009). Artaud's engagement with Eastern theatre, particularly Balinese performance, profoundly impacted his development of the Theatre of Cruelty. He admired how these performances conveyed emotions and narratives through physical movement and ritualistic elements, rather than relying heavily on dialogue, thus "inventing a language of gesture to be developed in space, a language without meaning except in the circumstances of the stage" (Artaud 1958: 61).

In *The Sense of Performance: Post-Artaud Theatre*, Susie J. Tharu explores the political and epistemological implications of Artaud's concept of the body as a medium. According to Tharu, Artaud presents the frenzied body as a sign that reveals "the sense or the lived meaning of that gesture" (Tharu 1984: 11) through its transformation of the act into the spectacular. Building on Artaud's ideas, Bausch's dance theatre regards the body as a canvas for social inscription, where the politics of gender are articulated through performative acts. The body serves as the center of a non-logocentric imaginary, expressed through dynamic and expressive movements (Price 1990: 323). This is particularly relevant to Tian's portrayal of the female body giving birth in the prologue.

Tian's direct influence from Artaud is evident in her statement, "I do not like plays where actors simply stand and talk; I hope the stage exudes energy through the actors' lines, mental states, and physical movements" (Tian 2003: 227). While Artaud inspired her conceptually, Bausch provided practical insights into the treatment of bodies on stage. *The Field of Life and Death* draws on the vocabulary of Bausch's dance theatre, emphasizing the release of physical movement, amplifying everyday actions, and highlighting the sculptural sense of the stage. This sculptural approach clarifies the boundary between life and art, enhancing the imaginative and expressive power of the performance. Tian required her actors to rigorously manage their visual presentation and engage in intense physicality. In *The Field of Life and Death*, the actors' performances are highly stylized. The characters' entrances are all sculptural, embodying the robust and earthy lives of northern farmers. The audience was particularly impressed by Ni Dahong's portrayal of Two-and-a-Half Li, characterized by his hunched posture, slightly bent legs, and the habitual gesture of keeping his hands tucked into his sleeves.

Tian's affinity for Antonin Artaud and Pina Bausch stems from her recognition of a profound connection between their theatrical languages and the traditional Chinese theatre. Her early experiences in traditional Chinese opera instilled in her a preference for stylized presentation and strong visual impact. This influence is evident in her stage designs, which employ a symbolic and minimalist style akin to traditional Chinese theatre.

In *The Field of Life and Death*, Tian's set design is highly symbolic and uses minimal props, allowing the actors' movements to take center stage. Most scenes feature earthen steps that evoke the northern Chinese landscape. A raised square wooden platform serves as the prison where Zhao San is confined, while a recessed square pit represents the cellar where Cheng Ye and Golden Bough hide. The recurring prop of the "pumpkin lantern" appears throughout the play, culminating in the final act as a ritualistic symbol conveying the theme of "sacrificing for survival." The minimalist set, free from the constraints of realism, requires the actors to use their actions to create the space, similar to the practices in Chinese traditional opera (Tian 2003: 216). This approach not only accentuates the actors' movements but also enhances the overall imaginative and expressive power of the performance. The immense success of *The Field of Life and Death* laid a solid foundation for Tian's later adaptations. Subsequently, each of her works has focused on integrating Western concepts with Chinese indigenous theatre.

2.2 Adapting Eileen Chang's *Red Rose, White Rose*: From Desolation on Page to Playfulness on Stage

In *Hooked: Art and Attachment*, Rita Felski examines the factors that draw people to art and cause them to form attachments to certain works. She theorizes people's connections with art through three attachment devices: attunement, identification, and interpretation. Attunement involves those often prelinguistic "affinities, inclinations, stirrings that often fall below the threshold of consciousness" (Felski 2020: xii), while identification is described as an "affinity based on some sense of similarity," an experience shared by both professional critics and lay readers, even when they "find different points of connection" (e.g., affective, political, philosophical) (Felski 2020: 81). In this sense, Tian appears more attuned and identified with Xiao Hong than with Eileen Chang (Zhang Ailing, 1920–1995), another prominent female writer from the period of the War of Resistance against Japan. This raises the question: Why did Tian undertake the adaptation of one of Chang's signature novellas, *Red Rose, White Rose*? This stage adaptation marked her alignment with the commercial turn of Chinese theatre in the twenty-first century, where artistic, entertaining, and city-oriented forms appeal to an urban audience. Moreover, Eileen Chang's works possess significant commercial appeal.

Chang was born into a declining aristocratic family in Shanghai. Her early life was marked by family turmoil, including her parents' separation and her father's addiction to opium. Despite these challenges, Chang demonstrated remarkable academic prowess, eventually attending the University of Hong Kong, where she studied literature. However, her education was interrupted by the Japanese occupation during World War II. Chang returned to Shanghai and began her literary career, quickly gaining recognition for her novellas and short stories that often explored themes of love, betrayal, and the complexities of human relationships. Between 1943 and 1944, Chang published notable novellas such as *The Golden Cangue*, *Love in a Fallen City*, and *Red Rose, White Rose*, which remain immensely popular among Chinese readers. In 1952, she relocated to Hong Kong and later to the United States, where she continued her writing career. Leading a reclusive life, Chang passed away on September 8, 1995, in Los Angeles.

In contrast to Xiao Hong, Eileen Chang's literary status in mainland China took a long and winding journey to consolidate. Unlike most of her contemporaries, who were deeply involved in the New Culture and nationalist movements, Chang's work focused on personal rather than national themes. The dramatic social upheavals of her time were merely background noise in her writings (Louie 2012a: 4–5). Another factor affecting her reception in mainland China was her association with Hu Lancheng, who served in Wang Jingwei's puppet government during the Japanese occupation. Although their marriage was brief and ended due to Hu's infidelity, both her connection to a Japanese collaborator and her insistence on remaining "apolitical" led to her being marginalized in mainland China until the 1980s.

The advancement of research on Eileen Chang was significantly propelled by American Chinese scholar C. T. Hsia's seminal work, *A History of Modern Chinese Fiction*, published in 1961. This landmark study marked Chang's first entry into the annals of Chinese literary history, with Hsia lauding her as "the best and most important writer in Chinese today" (389). In 1979, the Chinese translation of Hsia's book was published in Hong Kong, capturing the attention of mainland scholars in the early 1980s. This period coincided with the beginning of China's reform and opening up, facilitating increased exchanges between the mainland and Hong Kong. Many scholars brought back copies of Hsia's *A History of Modern Chinese Fiction* from Hong Kong, thereby bringing

Chang into the academic spotlight (Zhang 2012). This scholarly recognition was subsequently embraced and amplified by the film and media industries, introducing Chang to a vast audience of readers and viewers, and igniting the "Eileen Chang craze." Chang's apolitical stance, her skill in dissecting the minute details of mundane life and romantic love, and her vivid descriptions of Shanghai and Hong Kong, all resonated deeply with the tastes of Chinese urbanites during the reform and opening-up period. Although her works are imbued with a pervasive sense of melancholy and tragedy, which Chang herself described as *huangliang* (desolation), this mood evolved into an appealing aesthetic for the commercial consumption of China's urban dwellers. This was especially true of the urban dwellers labeled as *xiaozi* (the Chinese petty bourgeoisie), who aspire to a lifestyle of refined taste. Indeed, with numerous adaptations of her works appearing on stage and screen, Eileen Chang emerged as one of the most dazzling and successful cultural icons of the era (Wen 2004: 27).

As a native Beijinger, drawn to weighty, powerful works like Xiao Hong's *Field of Life and Death*, Tian admitted that she initially did not have much interest in Eileen Chang's writing. For Tian, Chang's focus on urban romance and personal trivialities lacked the broader depth found in Xiao Hong's work (Wang et al. 2010: 28). Her decision to adapt Chang's *Red Rose, White Rose* was influenced by the changing context of the Chinese theatre industry in the twenty-first century. At the beginning of the twenty-first century, globalization and state policies aimed at incorporating theatre into the cultural industry brought significant ideological, organizational, and performance diversity to the spoken theatre. The new NTC, where Tian has worked, was established in 2001 by merging the National Youth Art Theatre and the National Experimental Theatre, instituting a producer-driven system, which means "producers like Li Dong were to have more control over each production" (Chou 2016: 168). Since then, Tian has collaborated with Li to orchestrate savvy promotional campaigns for all her productions. Similarly, in South China, the Shanghai Dramatic Art Centre, formed in 1995 by merging the Shanghai People's Art Theatre and the Shanghai Qingnian Huaju Tuan (Shanghai Youth Huaju Company), developed a department under Yu Rongjun, a prolific playwright who has combined popular elements of 'white-collar theatre' for Shanghai's middle-class audience (Liu 2016: 327).

Tian expressed nostalgia for the socialist institutional framework of the 1990s. Reflecting on the changes within the theatre environment in China, she states:

> In the past ... commercial considerations were not a priority. The environment was relaxed, and we did not face the same pressures of daily life. It was

reminiscent of the Ming Dynasty playwright Tang Xianzu, who maintained his own troupe and performed his own plays . . . we did not have to worry about livelihood issues. Gathering a group of actors to create a play of my choosing was, of course, incredibly joyful. However, . . . we are indeed living through a period of dramatic change in China. In just a decade, I have personally experienced this transformation. I went from a state of contentment to suddenly feeling the increasing pressure of box office performance. The rules of success have shifted to a commercial paradigm where a director's ability to draw in box office revenue has become the ultimate marker of worldly success (Wang et al. 2010: 26–7).

In 2001, Tian was granted the opportunity to operate her own studio, with the arrangement that she would share the profits from the shows produced there with NTC (Chou 2016: 168). It was under such circumstances that Tian was persuaded by her producer to undertake the adaptation of *Red Rose, White Rose*, a project that other directors had struggled with and failed to complete. Following the remarkable box office success and a fifty-performance national tour of the first adaptation in 2008, she recognized the enduring profitability of Eileen Chang's works in today's market. Consequently, she also produced a contemporary version in 2010, setting the story in modern China to appeal to a younger audience. Tian noted that she undertook this project to support her team, particularly the younger members, who faced increasing financial pressures within the industry (Wang et al. 2010: 27). By October 2011, this updated version had already surpassed 120 performances.[13]

Chang's 1944 novella *Red Rose, White Rose* tells the story of Zhenbao, a diligent and ambitious young man from a modest background who earns a scholarship to study abroad. During his time overseas, he has his first sexual encounter with a French prostitute and later falls in love with a Eurasian girl named Rose. Upon returning to Shanghai, he secures a high-paying position at a foreign-owned textile factory. This job integrates him into the world of the middle class, and he starts a passionate affair with Wang Jiaorui (the Red Rose), the wife of his old friend Wang Shihong. Ultimately, fearing his "mother's tears," Zhenbao chooses his career over romance, ending his relationship with Jiaorui and marrying a frigid yet socially acceptable woman named Meng Yanli (the White Rose). The lack of sexual attraction in their marriage prompts him to visit prostitutes regularly as a reward for his sacrifices for his family and society. As Zhenbao grows increasingly estranged from his family, he encounters Jiaorui, now a respectable mother, and begins to lament his life choices. Meanwhile, he discovers that his wife is having an affair with a tailor. The

---

[13] The analysis of Tian's adaptation of this play is based on the first production in 2008.

story concludes with Zhenbao reaffirming his roles as an honorable husband, responsible father, and respectable citizen.

In Tian's adaptation, the play opens with Tong Zhenbao's discovery of his wife's affair, triggering a series of past recollections of his romantic encounter with Jiaorui, the Red Rose, interspersed with current events and flashbacks. A glass corridor is placed in the center, with the apartments of the Red and White Roses on either side. The intense contrast between the two spaces and the different "roses" forms the core structure and energy of the play. As Tong Zhenbao alternates between the two apartments, the past and present events interweave. Tian later explained, "the apartments are like a man's heart: the left atrium and the right atrium, one for the lover and one for the wife. The glass corridor is the phallus or vagina" (Tian 2010a: 183). When Zhenbao is caught between the two apartments, and between the present and the past, he constantly passes through the corridor, symbolizing his conflict between reality and desire.

Another innovative design that enhances the dramatic tension and excitement is the split selves. The three main characters – Zhenbao, the Red Rose, and the White Rose – are each portrayed by two identically costumed actors: one representing the character's outer persona and the other their inner emotions. All actors remain on stage together throughout the play. This creative choice enables each character to engage in self-argument, self-criticism, self-advice, and sometimes reenacting scenes (Melvin 2008). For instance,

Tong Zhenbao: Don't fall in love with Wang Jiaorui; she's a married woman!

Zhenbao B: Her face is beautiful and smooth.

Tong Zhenbao: Her husband is my old classmate, my old friend.

Zhenbao B: Her body, every curve, every inch, is full of life.

Tong Zhenbao: I, Tong Zhenbao, am a man of virtue who remains unmoved by temptation (Tian 2010b: 76).

Tian explains that she found inspiration in Eileen Chang's depiction of Tong Zhenbao as being "simultaneously regretful and resolute" when abandoning the Red Rose (Tian 2010a: 186). The use of two actors for a single role is an ingenious move that directly expresses much of the subtext from the original work. It also adds a playful element akin to traditional Chinese *xiangsheng* (crosstalk), where two performers engage in humorous banter and debate, creating both conflict and laughter. This lively stage presentation avoids the dullness often found in film adaptations of Chang's works, which, while faithful and visually appealing, can be quite somber. Tian admits that she aimed to escape the shadow of the "artistic but dull" film by Stanley Kwan, who directed the film *Red Rose, White Rose* in 1994 (Tian 2010a: 183).

To further engage the audience, she incorporated widely known quotes by Eileen Chang from her other works, asking the actors to deliver them in a meta-theatrical manner. For example, in the play, the White Rose says, "To capture a man's heart, you must first capture his stomach. To capture a woman's heart, you must pass through her vagina. Eileen Chang said so" (Tian 2010b: 90).

Furthermore, in Tian's stage adaptation, the dialogues between Tong Zhenbao and Zhenbao B sometimes become overly explicit, exposing too much subtext and imposing value judgments on the audience. It is actually much more enjoyable for a reader to read between the lines than to see everything spelled out on stage. For example,

Zhenbao B: You're wrong! Love and desire are inseparable. That was your cowardice. You wanted to be a paragon of virtue. Because she was Wang Shihong's wife, you didn't dare marry her. You cared about society's view and your mother's tears.

Tong Zhenbao: Of course, I cared about my mother's tears. I come from humble beginnings. I built my world with my own hands. Without a good reputation, I couldn't stand at the forefront of the world. I wouldn't have a bright future.

Zhenbao B: You finally admit it. For your bright future . . .

Zhenbao B: Ultimately, it's because you're selfish.

Tong Zhenbao: No, I'm not selfish . . . I'm selfless. For social responsibility, for my mother's tears, for my family, I sacrificed my desires, my freedom, and myself. (Tian 2010b: 113)

Apart from the danger of "telling" too much, the playfulness of the adapted version overshadows the tragic and desolate undertone of the original work, as Sheila Melvin comments, "Romantic moments are rendered humorous as they become ménage à trois or quatre, and tragic scenes are undercut by the farcical nature of the characters' second-guessing of their own motives, and the physical presence of four actors instead of two" (Melvin 2008).

The use of two actors for one character reinforces the dichotomy of the original work. In the novella, there are many dichotomies, including the structure, characters, and imagery. The story is almost neatly divided into two halves, with the first half describing Zhenbao's affair with Jiaorui and the second half his marriage to Yanli and his growing moral disintegration. The most striking dichotomy is the "red rose"/"white rose" distinction. This, in turn, matches the dichotomy between "Chinese" and "Western" in both men and women. The Red

Rose is passionate and impulsive, while the White Rose is restrained and conservative. The Red Rose character Wang Jiaorui is a Singaporean who was educated in England, while Zhenbao's wife, the White Rose Meng Yanli, is a traditional Chinese woman from a good family (Louie 2012b: 27). Readers are captivated by the ingenious metaphors involving the Red Rose and the White Rose. In the novella, every man is said to face this choice at least once in his life, and neither option leads to true happiness: A Red Rose, if married, will become a "mosquito-blood streak smeared on the wall," while a White Rose will turn into "a grain of sticky rice that's gotten stuck to your clothes" (Chang 2007: 8).

Rey Chow, however, contends that the dichotomy between the Red Rose and the White Rose does more than reflect the male protagonist Zhenbao's objectification of women – it also reveals his broader worldview. Chow notes that, "if we focus solely on the 'Red Rose' and 'White Rose' as metaphors for the female characters, we miss something crucial. The polarization of these two terms distracts us from the fact that the women in Zhenbao's life are interchangeable, replaceable objects" (Chow 1999: 163). This interpretation adds layers of irony to Eileen Chang's depiction of men's perceived choice between the two figures. Chang's novella, rather than merely presenting the conflict between the passionate Red Rose and the restrained White Rose, fundamentally critiques the moral decay of men in Shanghai on the cusp of modernity in the early twentieth century (Louie 2012a: 7). In the end, Zhenbao is reintegrated into society as a "good person," but this "goodness" is defined within the framework of traditional Chinese Confucian values, combined with the Western ideal of the self-made man. Both systems prioritize responsibility, decency, and self-restraint over passion and romantic love. Therefore, the contrast between the Red and White Roses – wildly passionate versus deathly restrained – mirrors Zhenbao's internal conflict (Louie 2012b: 29). In Tian's adaptation, this internal conflict seems to be resolved by the character Tong Zhenbao killing Zhenbao B, thereby completing his symbolic transformation into a White Rose.

Tian's adaptation of Eileen Chang's work successfully avoids the pitfall of being "artistic but dull." Yet, in doing so, it sacrifices much of the original's complexity and irony. While the playful elements undoubtedly contribute to the commercial success of the production, they ultimately overshadow the underlying sense of desolation that is central to Chang's theme. The scholar of modern Chinese literature, Wen Rumin, notes that the surge of interest in Eileen Chang beginning in the 1990s, fueled by film and television adaptations in popular culture, has gradually eroded the rich complexities of her work. In this ongoing cultural production, the figure of "Eileen Chang" has been reduced to a refined commodity, stripped of much of its depth (Wen 2004: 27). Clearly, Tian has also been a part of this cultural production.

2.3 Adapting Lilian Lee Pik-Wah's *Green Snake*: Female Desire and Tian's Playful Theatrics

Tian Qinxin's adaptation of *Green Snake*, based on Lee Pik-Wah's novel *Green Snake*, premiered on March 21, 2013 at the Opera House of the Hong Kong Academy for Performing Arts. This production continued and expanded upon the playful and meta-theatrical techniques she had explored in her earlier adaptation of *Red Rose, White Rose*.

The *Legend of the White Snake*, one of China's most enduring and cherished folk tales, has evolved significantly over the centuries, reflecting the changing cultural, religious, and social currents of Chinese society. Though its roots lie in oral traditions, the story gained literary prominence during the Song and Yuan dynasties, where it began to transform from a cautionary tale of a serpent demon into a richly layered narrative of love, loyalty, and transcendence.

The Ming dynasty marked a pivotal moment in the tale's development, particularly through the work of Feng Menglong (1574–1646). His 1624 version, *Bai niangzi yongzhen Leifengta (*Madame White Imprisoned Forever under Thunder Peak Pagoda*)*, solidified the narrative's place in Chinese cultural history. The story begins with Xu Xian, a young pharmacist, encountering the enchanting Madame White by West Lake on a rainy day. Their brief meeting, during which Xu Xian lends her his umbrella, quickly blossoms into love, leading to their marriage and the opening of a herbal medicine shop with Madame White's assistance. However, during the Dragon Boat Festival, the monk Fa Hai, who possesses formidable exorcist powers, discovers Madame White's true identity as a white snake spirit. Shocked and terrified, Xu Xian turns to Fa Hai for help, seeking refuge from Madame White and her sister, Little Green (the Green Snake). In the end, Fa Hai imprisons Madame White under the Thunder Peak Pagoda, condemning her to eternal captivity.

Later adaptations of the legend shifted the portrayal of Madame White (the White Snake), transforming her from a feared antagonist into a sympathetic protagonist. As Taryn Li-Min Chun notes, "Narratively, dramatic adaptation tends to humanize the demonic Madame White by making her more compassionate toward the people around her" (Chun 2019: 308). In subsequent retellings, Madame White and Little Green wage a fierce battle against Fa Hai and his followers to rescue Xu Xian. In these later versions, Madame White even becomes pregnant and gives birth to a fully human child, symbolizing her ultimate integration into the human world.

In her comprehensive and transnational study, *The Global White Snake*, Luo Liang explores the complex interplay of bodily transformation, divine metamorphosis, identity, and belonging in the evolution of the White Snake legend.

Luo argues that the pursuit of humanity and womanhood lies at the heart of these shifting narratives (Luo 2021:261). She further observes that in contemporary China, the humanization of the White Snake is mirrored by the enduring animalistic traits of the Green Snake. The Green Snake's rebellious and indulgent nature has increasingly come to the forefront, evolving from a secondary character into a prominent and radically transgressive figure. Luo suggests that this transformation resonates deeply with the anti-traditional spirit and experimental tendencies of both China's revolutionary era and its postmodern context (Luo 2021: 261).

Hong Kong writer Lee Pik-Wah (1959–) is often regarded as a pioneering figure in the modern reinterpretation of the *Legend of the White Snake*, particularly through her exploration of the Green Snake character. Her novel *Green Snake*, originally written in the late 1980s and revised in the early 1990s, reimagines the relationships between Fa Hai, Xu Xian, Madame White, and Little Green, shifting the narrative focus to the younger Green Snake. Lee, also known as Li Bihua, is a prolific author and screenwriter, celebrated for her ability to intertwine Chinese folklore with contemporary themes. Her works often explore the complexities of identity, gender, and the supernatural, making her a distinctive voice in Hong Kong literature and cinema. Many of her works have been adapted into films and received widespread acclaim, such as *Farewell My Concubine*, *Rouge*, and *Green Snake*. At the premiere of *Green Snake*, Tian remarked that she had been invited by Li Bihua five years earlier and had long considered approaching the work from a somewhat different perspective in her adaptation (Niu 2012).

In *Green Snake*, Lee reinterprets the traditional narrative by centering the story on Little Green, offering a fresh perspective on the legend. The novel portrays Green Snake as a more transgressive and multifaceted character, whose relationship with Madame White is marked by both loyalty and rivalry. Through this shift in perspective, Lee challenges the conventional moral binaries of the original tale, presenting instead a nuanced exploration of desire, freedom, and the quest for self-identity within the constraints of both human and supernatural realms. The novel was adapted into a Cantonese film by Tsui Hark (1950–) in 1993, which further popularized the Green Snake-centered narrative within the legend.

Tian's theatre adaptation of Lee's novel, twenty years later, takes an even more drastic approach to accentuate the Green Snake's sexual awakening and her relentless pursuit of freedom to love. On their path to humanity, two sister snakes embodying contrasting extremes of Chinese femininity both experience love and lust. Once in a woman's form, the White Snake learns human language, adopts human gestures, and follows traditional moral values, becoming the ideal Confucian wife and mother dedicated to family and duty. In sharp contrast, the Green Snake resists the constraints of societal expectations, boldly expressing her sexual desires through her newly assumed female body. Tian's adaptation adds scenes where the Green Snake indulges in passionate sexual encounters with various characters – such as a constable, a blacksmith, a vegetable seller, and a tailor – most provocatively with the monk Fa Hai. In a striking scene, she approaches him at Jinshan Temple, declaring, "Monk, I want to sleep with you" (Tian and An 2013: 21)! When the White Snake urges her to be faithful to one man, the Green Snake retorts, "I like what I like; why must it be for life? I am a serpent, not like them. I don't want to follow the rules of humans, nor do I wish to be as cautious as my older sister. I am a snake that can transform into a person, and I like who I am" (Tian and An 2013: 23). This monstrosity within her becomes a potent force driving her pursuit of freedom.

Critics have observed that Tian, for the first time in her plays, centers on female sexual desire. Tian explains that for much of her career, she worked within the confines of a framework established by a dominant gender, constantly striving to embody the same qualities, such as spatial awareness and strength. However, it was through her work on *Green Snake* that her female consciousness began to resurface, as she sought to give voice to a woman's innermost thoughts (Zhou and Huang 2013).

If Lee offers a revisionist rewriting of *Green Snake*, then Tian provides a revisionist portrayal of the Buddhist monk Fa Hai, a character traditionally depicted as an elderly, inflexible, and heartless moral guardian who breaks apart the happy marriage between the White Snake and her human husband. In Tian's adaptation, Fa Hai is reimagined as a young, talented man on the path to Buddhist enlightenment. Rather than simply presenting him as a great villain, Tian explores his struggles with the temptations and suffering inherent in the Buddhist journey, particularly his complex feelings of love for the Green Snake. Tian has stated that her growing interest in Buddhism influenced her decision to frame the story within the three realms of human experience, monstrosity, and Buddhahood (Zhou and Huang 2013). As the Green Snake's sexual desire becomes unrestrained and ultimately self-destructive, the play suggests that the fact that female sexual desire can defy societal conventions does not preclude it from being an obstacle to that ultimate freedom that can be attained through Buddhist practices. Both Fa Hai and the Green Snake undergo their own forms of spiritual growth. By the play's conclusion, Fa Hai decides to remain in the human realm to help others, including offering salvation to the Green Snake. Though she continues to love him, the Green Snake merely watches Fa Hai from the beams of Jinshan Temple, no longer harassing him.

After Fa Hai's nirvana, the Green Snake, having completed her own spiritual practice, becomes a mortal with a finite lifespan (Liu 2019: 10).

Although the play addresses themes of desire and salvation, it also retains elements of playfulness and meta-theatricality that appeal to modern Chinese audiences. As previously noted in the discussion of Tian's adaptations of *Red Rose, White Rose*, her "playful theatrics" draw on the traditions of Chinese theatre. At the beginning of the play, Fa Hai introduces himself in a manner typical of classical performance: "I am Fa Hai, one of the characters in the *Legend of the White Snake*. I am the presiding monk of Jinshan Temple, the head of the temple, a very young leader" (Tian and An 2013: 10). He further announces, "The story is purely fictional, based on a folk tale passed down for six hundred years" (Tian and An 2013: 10). This self-referential design applies to most of the characters in Tian's adaptation, allowing them to step in and out of the narrative. This creates a distancing effect and invites them to speak directly to the audience, prompting reflection or laughter. For instance, the Green Snake tells Fa Hai, "Your *Legend of the White Snake* is probably wrong. It's been misrepresented for years!" When Fa Hai replies, "My version was written by Feng Menglong during the Ming Dynasty," the Green Snake retorts, "I will rewrite it!" (Tian and An 2013: 48) (see Figure 5).

As a revisionist figure in Tian's adaptation, Fa Hai frequently steps out of the play to voice his discontent with previous narratives. He sometimes quips, "Until I was written into the *Legend of the White Snake*, my duty was simply to exorcise demons. But is my role to exorcise demons, or to be compassionate? It's all a bit confusing" (Tian and An 2013: 11). On other occasions, he defends

Figure 5 Little Green and Monk Fa Hai in *Green Snake*. Screenshot by the author from the recorded performance *Green Snake, Bilibili*, www.bilibili.com/video/BV14Z8eziETx?p=7. Accessed October 15, 2025.

himself, saying, "This is how my good name has been ruined" (Tian and An 2013: 51). These moments often elicit hearty laughter from the audience. The play's playfulness and comedic effect are further enhanced by a rich mix of dialects, classical Chinese, modern language, vernacular, and Sichuanese, adding layers of humor and appeal for the audience.

Nelson Pressley remarked on Tian's *Green Snake* at the Kennedy Center in Washington, DC, in 2014, "It's a pleasing eyeful, and a playful blend of old and new" (Pressley 2014). The production drew on stage conventions of Chinese opera while incorporating an international design team of German scenic, Chinese multimedia, and British lighting designers (Shui 2013). Minimalist in form, the set echoed the aesthetics of a traditional opera stage with a single screen, yet it fully exploited the power of suggestion, allowing the audience to imagine shifting locations from the "Broken Bridge" where Bai Suzhen meets Xu Xian, to Xu Xian's home, Jinshan Temple, and the Lei Feng Pagoda. The characters, travelling from place to place, often generate new storylines, keeping the plot in a fluid and dynamic state, rather than being confined to one environment. In the final act, the setting shifts from the Song Dynasty to the modern era, with the main characters wearing contemporary clothes and encountering each other in present-day society. This temporal shift is thematically significant, and its smooth integration with the overall aesthetic ensures it is easily accepted by theatre audiences familiar with the conventions of Chinese opera. The time-travel element is made plausible within the play's framework, as the audience has already agreed to the temporal and spatial assumptions established by the performance style.

Moreover, the play frequently uses stylized movements from Chinese opera. Tian deconstructs these traditional movements into symbolic gestures, allowing the audience to recognize familiar elements from Chinese opera while maintaining a natural integration with the narrative. For example, in *Green Snake*, Tian cast two actors, Qin Hailu and Yuan Quan, both with a background in Peking opera, to play the Green and White Snakes. They incorporate the traditional Peking opera movements into their performances – stepping in small, delicate strides, while keeping their upper bodies perfectly still, evoking the snake's form and inner sensuality. When embodying the laziness of the snakes, they can quickly slither across the stage. The Green Snake, in particular, expresses her intense sexual desire through gestures such as "entwining" and "licking." The White Snake imitates the "cloud step" in the Peking opera, gliding across the stage with a smooth, ethereal quality, creating a haunting presence. When the white snake discovers that the Green Snake and Xu Xian have developed feelings for each other, the confrontation between the two sister snakes is expressed through an abstract, Tai Chi-inspired fan dance.

The visual appeal and comic elements of Tian's adaptation contributed significantly to its continued popularity. Following its premiere in Hong Kong on March 21, 2013, *Green Snake* toured several cities from 2013 to 2014, including Beijing, Shanghai, Taipei, Macau, Shenzhen, and Foshan, garnering widespread attention. In 2014, the production participated in four prestigious international arts festivals, including the Edinburgh Festival Fringe, the Hong Kong Arts Festival, the Shanghai International Arts Festival, and the Kennedy Center American Theater Festival. By the end of October 2014, it was selected as the opening production of the second Wuzhen Theatre Festival. For this special occasion, the play was redesigned, marking the first-ever outdoor water theatre production in China. The water theatre version of *Green Snake* proved to be a dazzling spectacle. Additionally, Tian incorporated digital performance elements, such as multimedia installations, to craft a stage experience with a distinctly cinematic quality.

Green Snake is Tian's most unabashedly woman-centered venture: It puts female desire at the center – not as a moral lapse but as a source of insight and agency, and lets playfulness puncture piety. With a spare, suggestive stage grammar and a nimble mix of dialects and operatic gesture, the legend moves with contemporary ease while retaining ritual weight.

3 Adapting Chinese Classics and Shakespeare

This section examines Tian Qinxin's reinterpretations of two Chinese classics alongside her radical reworking of Shakespeare's *King Lear* (2008). It opens with *The Orphan of Zhao* (2003), analyzing how Tian reframes the protagonists to embody contemporary rather than feudal Confucian values. It then turns to her staging of Lao She's modern novel *The Yellow Storm* (2010), highlighting the balance she strikes among nationalist ideology, artistic craft, and commercial appeal within the main-melody paradigm. Tian's collaboration with producer Li Dong is also considered a window onto her directorial method. The discussion culminates in *Ming* (2008), Tian's *Lear* relocated to the Ming dynasty and rendered in a postmodern, parodic register designed for audience engagement and ease. Read together, these works align with – and in places anticipate – the later injunction to "tell China's stories well," as Tian, increasingly integrated with cultural institutions, mobilizes classical legacies and revolutionary narratives for contemporary stages. Across the corpus, her adaptations reveal a deft negotiation between seriousness and play, and between inherited forms and modern sensibilities.

In *The Orphan of Zhao*, Tian sets aside the traditional revenge arc to foreground *cheng xin* (sincerity and trust 诚信), which she regards as urgently lacking today. Returning to the Zuo Commentary, she recasts Princess Zhuangji not as a "chaste wife" but as a sexually assertive figure whose slander triggers catastrophe and whose childbirth becomes a crucible of ethical awakening as she entrusts her baby to Cheng Ying before taking her own life. Onstage, this moral turn is visualised through red-and-black expressionism (vein-like motifs, hinging black panels), Artaud-inflected physical scores and sculptural pauses, and operatic sign systems – soldiers circling with a sword and red bundle to signify massacre – coalescing into stark tableaux that externalize desire, shame, and resolve.

In *The Yellow Storm*, Tian demonstrates robust theatrical adaptation: She compresses Lao She's sprawling epic into a taut three-act structure focused on three families, threads a storyteller through the action, and uses a seasonal arc as the narrative spine. Her "new realism" design conjures an ethnographic Old Beijing via a movable hutong and an open central playing space. The production advances a home-and-nation unity consonant with main-melody culture while avoiding blunt didacticism.

Tian's *Ming* (a retitled, relocated *King Lear*) was conceived with a clear commercial aim: leveraging the popular "Ming" brand and a bestselling IP to localize Shakespeare and broaden the audience. The adaptation shifts Lear's tragic ethics into a palace-intrigue succession game, with Zhu Yuanzhang coldly engineering rivalry among his sons – an overt turn from filial tragedy to court scheming. Drawing playful energy from *xiqu* conventions – meta-theatrical self-introductions, fluid stepping in and out of role, onstage costume changes, tea-table asides, and folk-comic routines – Tian privileges performative pleasure over canonical solemnity, a choice that invites questions about narrative fragmentation and the limits of this playful, localized approach.

3.1 Adapting *The Orphan of Zhao*: Historicity and Contemporaneity

In 2003, thirty-four-year-old Tian Qinxin traveled to Taiwan with the esteemed director Lin Zhaohua (1936–). During their visit, they attended a performance of the Peking opera *The Orphan of Zhao*, which inspired both to consider adapting the story for the modern stage. This moment was pivotal for Tian, who was then emerging as a younger voice in Chinese theatre and seeking to establish her artistic identity through bold reinterpretations of classical material. Upon their return, Lin secured the support of the Beijing People's Art Theater for his production, assembling a stellar cast that included prominent actors such as Pu Cunxin, He Bing, and Xu Fan – leading actors in the realm of spoken drama at the time. When Tian learned of this, she hesitated, aware that her own project might be overshadowed by Lin's prestige. Yet her producer, Li Dong, urged her to seize the opportunity, arguing that even in competition with such an illustrious director she had much to gain: If successful, her talent would be recognized; if not, the attempt itself would demonstrate ambition. Encouraged by this support, Tian chose to proceed with her adaptation (Wang 2011). Thus, in 2003, two of China's foremost theatre institutions – the Beijing People's Art Theatre, where Lin was a veteran, and the National Theater of China, where Tian served as a director – staged rival productions of *The Orphan of Zhao* in Beijing, sparking considerable attention among playgoers and critics and situating Tian directly in dialogue with one of the giants of Chinese theatre.

The tale of the Orphan of Zhao has endured for nearly 3,000 years, originating in the Spring and Autumn period (770–468 BC) of China. Initially recorded in *The Spring and Autumn Annals*, it was later developed into a more cohesive narrative in *The Zuo Commentary*: During the reign of the tyrannical Duke Ling of Jin, Minister Zhao Dun repeatedly cautioned him, leading to their enmity. After Zhao Dun's nephew killed the duke, Zhao Dun supported the ascension of Duke Cheng, strengthening the Zhao family's power. Zhao Dun's son, Zhao Shuo, married Princess Zhuangji, the duke's daughter. When Zhuangji engaged in an affair and falsely accused the Zhao family of treason, Duke Jing, seeking to diminish the influence of his ministers, ordered the execution of the entire Zhao clan. Only Zhao Wu, the son of Zhao Shuo, survived due to his mother's protection. Later, Duke Jing, persuaded by others, pardoned Zhao Wu and restored his status.

Although the initial account is brief, it hints at the intense political struggles of the time, yet lacks the themes of revenge and tragedy that later versions would emphasize, as well as clear delineations between opposing sides. In the first century BC, historian Sima Qian recounted this story in his *Records of the Grand Historian*, omitting the details of Zhuangji's slander and introducing the antagonist Tu'an Gu, who is driven by ambition and jealousy to seek revenge against the Zhao family. Acting without Duke Jing's consent, he attacks the Zhao clan, annihilating them. Another key figure introduced is Cheng Ying, a retainer of the Zhao family, who, along with another retainer, Gongsun Chuju, devises a plan to save the orphan Zhao Wu by substituting another infant. Cheng Ying deliberately accuses Gongsun of harboring the orphan, leading to the deaths of both Gongsun and the child, while he raises Zhao Wu in hiding. Fifteen years later, alerted by General Han Jue, Duke Jing uncovers the truth. Han Jue then finds Cheng Ying and Zhao Wu and launches an assault on the Tu family. Zhao Wu's titles and lands are restored, but Cheng Ying commits suicide after Zhao Wu reaches adulthood, thereby fulfilling his feudal duty to follow his lord to the grave. The accounts in *The Zuo Commentary* and the *Records of the Grand Historian* reflect significant variations in characters and events, highlighting differing societal contexts; the former emphasizes the struggle between aristocratic and monarchical power, while the latter foregrounds Confucian values of loyalty and righteousness.[14] When Tian revisited the textual history of the story, she was struck by how each retelling, whether concise or expansive, reflected the political and ethical concerns of its age. For her, the task of adapting the piece in the twenty-first century was precisely to reframe its moral focus for a contemporary audience. As she explains, the aim was to "construct an imagined ancient world of our own creation" (Tian 2010b: 129).

The story of orphan Zhao has been celebrated through the ages, evolving into a dramatic form by the thirteenth century during the Yuan dynasty. In Yuan drama, Confucian values were emphasized, magnifying the emotional impact of the tragedy. Cheng Ying no longer substitutes a nobody's infant for Zhao Wu but instead offers his own son. When Tu'an Gu learns of Zhao Wu's concealment, he issues a decree reminiscent of King Herod from the Bible: If Zhao Wu is not surrendered, all male infants under six months in Jin will be executed. In this drama, four characters, represented by Cheng Ying, embody different levels of loyalty and self-sacrifice: Cheng Ying, as a retainer, seeks to repay the Zhao family; Gongsun Chuju, now an elder returning to retirement, sacrifices himself to ensure the success of the substitution plan out of loyalty to Zhao Dun; Zhuangji commits suicide after entrusting her son to Cheng Ying, wishing to join her deceased husband; and Han Jue, although initially aligned with Tu'an Gu, acts on moral conviction to free Cheng Ying and Zhao Wu, ultimately taking his own life. Moreover, Zhao Wu's quest for vengeance is rooted in dual Confucian values: on a personal level, seeking retribution for his family, and on a public level, responding to Tu'an Gu's explicit treasonous intentions from the outset (Yu 2005: 133). In addition to promoting Confucian ideals, Yuan drama incorporates melodramatic elements of popular theatre. For example, Tu'an Gu secretly trains a fierce dog to attack a straw figure of Zhao Dun, bringing it into the palace to claim the dog could identify traitors; and, after being saved by Cheng Ying, Tu'an Gu mistakenly believes Zhao Wu to be Cheng Ying's son, adopting him and raising him as his own. Ultimately, Tu'an Gu is punished, suffering a gruesome execution for his regicide. Despite the numerous tragic events, the drama concludes in the traditional Chinese theatrical style of resolution: Zhao Wu avenges his family, restoring their status and fortune, while Cheng Ying, instead of taking his own life, kneels in gratitude alongside Zhao Wu to thank the king.

---

[14] For a detailed analysis of the differences between the accounts in the *Records of the Grand Historian* and the *Zuo Commentary*, see Lu, Xinsheng. 2020. "An Aesthetic Analysis of the Historical Writing of the 'Orphan of the Zhao Family' – A Discussion on the 'Objectivity' of History." *Journal of Shaanxi Normal University* 3 : 57–71.

For Tian, such material presented both an opportunity and a problem: The rich theatricality of Yuan drama offered compelling stage imagery, yet the stark Confucian emphasis on revenge and feudal duty risked alienating contemporary audiences. Her adaptation thus had to negotiate between reverence for tradition and the critical questioning of its values. The Yuan Drama became the first Chinese play to be translated into European languages (French, English, and Italian) during the Chinoiserie craze of the eighteenth century. Since then, countless adaptations have emerged, appearing in various forms, including Chinese and Western operas, films, radio dramas, novels, and plays.[15] As Shiao-Ling Yu observes, *The Orphan of Zhao* is perhaps the best-known drama of revenge in Chinese literature (Yu 2005: 129). The Orphan's revenge represents the coming together of the two cardinal Confucian virtues of loyalty (zhong 忠) and filial piety (xiao 孝). However, both Tian and Lin's adaptations rejected the theme of revenge as inconsistent with contemporary values. For example, dismissing the Orphan's revenge and the sacrifices made by the others as feudal nonsense, Lin made significant changes in the plot and characterization. Unlike the orphan who turns on his foster father without a moment's hesitation, and in some versions kills him with his own hands, Lin's modern orphan faces the dilemma of whether to avenge his father's death or to repay the kindness of his foster father. In this way, the orphan's concern has shifted from fulfilling his filial (and political) obligations to living his own life without any such moral burden (Yu 2005: 138–9).

In a similar vein, Tian's adaptation also neutralizes the theme of revenge. The play subverts the traditional linear narrative with flashbacks and juxtapositions

---

[15] During the late eighteenth century, amidst Europe's *Chinoiserie* craze, the Yuan dynasty play *The Orphan of Zhao* was translated into European languages by the Jesuit father Joseph Henri Marie de Prémare, making a significant impact. Figures like Goethe and Voltaire both used the story of *The Orphan of Zhao* as the basis for their own theatrical works, with Voltaire's *The Chinese Orphan* having the greatest influence. Since the twenty-first century, the play's impact has extended beyond Europe, breaking regional boundaries. In 2003, Chinese-American director Chen Shizheng adapted both Chinese and English versions of *The Orphan of Zhao*, which were performed at the Lincoln Center Festival in New York. In 2009, the opera *The Orphan of Zhao*, composed by Chinese-American composer Jeffery Ching, was staged at the Erfurt Theatre in Germany. In 2012, the Royal Shakespeare Company adapted and performed a stage version in the UK. In 2014, the National Theatre of Korea staged *The Orphan of Zhao: Seeds of Revenge*, directed by Ko Seon-hong, which was later performed in October 2016 at the NTC. Since the twenty-first century, adaptations of *The Orphan of Zhao* within China have spanned various forms. Regional opera adaptations include Henan opera *Cheng Ying Saves the Orphan* (2002, written by Chen Yongquan), Yue opera *The Orphan of Zhao* (2005, written by Yu Qingfeng), and Han opera *The Lost Son* (2015, written by Zheng Huaixing). Theatrical adaptations include Lin Zhaohua's version *The Orphan of Zhao* (2003, written by Jin Haishu) and Tian Qinxin's version *The Orphan of Zhao* (2003, written by Tian Qinxin). Film and television adaptations include Chen Kaige's 2010 film *The Orphan of Zhao*, and Yan Jiangang's 2013 41-episode TV series *The Orphan of Zhao*. Additionally, opera adaptations include Zhou Jingzhi's *The Orphan of Zhao* (2011) and Mo Fan's *The Orphan of Zhao* (2011).

of different time periods. It opens with the Orphan's dream and his lament on his sixteenth birthday: "I dreamt of my mother, I dreamt of her. Her red hair was flowing ... I never saw my mother. She died when she gave birth to me. Today, I am sixteen. In these sixteen years, I have only seen my father; I have two fathers" (Tian 2010b: 124). Then, his two elderly fathers, Cheng Ying and Tu'an Gu, each recount the events of sixteen years ago from their own perspectives. The orphan, torn between their conflicting accounts of his family's fate, is consumed by confusion. This dilemma imbues his character with a Hamlet-like hesitation, as he mourns, "I cannot bear to look at my father's wound, nor face his gaze. I am lost. Father, foster father ... which way should I go" (Tian 2010b: 163)? While the orphan in traditional versions is portrayed as resolute and decisive, Tian's version presents him as a bewildered, confused teenager, incapable of taking action. When he learns of his family's tragic fate, he is left utterly lost, not by a desire for revenge, but by the uncertainty of how to navigate his life (Yu 2005: 143).

The boldest change in Tian's adaptation is her return to the oldest narrative as recorded in *The Zuo Commentary*, particularly regarding Princess Zhuangji's slander. Tian strips the princess of the chaste wife guise given to her by the other playwrights, and portrays her as a wanton woman who proudly declares, "I am the duke of Jin's daughter; I can have any man I want" (Tian 2010b: 128). She does not realize, however, that her accusation would lead to tragic consequences: the killing of her father (Duke Ling) by the Zhaos and the massacre of the Zhao clan. The birth of her son under such traumatic circumstances becomes a turning point in the life of this arrogant princess. Confronted with a tragedy of her own making, she is determined to find a reliable person to raise her baby so he will grow up to continue the family line. She summons Cheng Ying, a humble country doctor, to her residence and begs him to take her child: "In this palace where the living live among the dead, I gave birth to this blood-covered baby. I felt pain but I dared not scream ... I wanted to cry but I had no tears. Doctor, please grant me my request" (Tian 2010b: 136). Moved by a mother's love for her child, Cheng Ying accepts her request. As he leaves with the baby, she kills herself.

Although the narrative attributing the massacre of Zhao Dun's family to the debauchery of Princess Zhuangji seems to reinforce the stereotype of women as the source of misfortune (often found in traditional Chinese stories), Tian offers a fresh interpretation. She suggests that Zhuangji's experience of childbirth, through the pain of labor, enabled her to mature into motherhood. It was through this process that she came to understand shame, recognize her own culpability, and achieve growth (Tian 2010b: 138).

In addition to incorporating contemporary perspectives, such as the confused orphan and the repentant mother, Tian portrays Cheng Ying in a different light. No longer a retainer of the Zhao family, indebted to them for his life and gratitude, in Tian's version Cheng Ying is simply a country doctor unbound by any obligation to the Zhao family. Out of compassion, Cheng Ying accepts Zhuangji's dying request and promises to treat the orphan as his own child. From that moment, and until his death, he remains true to this promise. His example also inspires others to follow suit. General Han Jue commits suicide to ensure the safe passage of both the Orphan and Cheng Ying, declaring that "in this chaotic world it is not easy to meet a gentleman of good faith" (Tian 2010b: 146). As Yu notes, "Cheng Ying emerges as a moral giant, and the virtue he represents is not blind loyalty but *cheng xin* (sincerity and trust)" (Yu 2005: 146). The contemporary term *cheng xin* is repeated more than a dozen times throughout the play, reflecting Tian's anxiety about the moral decline in Chinese society amidst overwhelming commercialization at the dawn of the twenty-first century.

Tian herself explains, "In today's society, moral values are in decline, and we are in a period of confusion regarding the reconstruction of values. Facing such a reality, I can use historical events to reflect on the present" (Dai 2004). She goes on to articulate her well-known sentiment:

> I create theatre because I am saddened. I am saddened by the chaos of today's society, the spread of selfish desires, the near collapse of moral ground, the obliteration of thought, and the loss of manners. The rampant monopolies and conquests, the overwhelming competition that stirs emotional confusion and anxiety to the point where people can no longer distinguish right from wrong. The gap between individuals is growing deeper, and even when someone shows kindness, we wonder whether they have some ulterior motive ... I create theatre because I am saddened ... Let us construct a stage – a fictive society built on imagination – this society encapsulates my sorrow in 2003 (Tian 2010b: 151).

In this sense, through her portrayal of Cheng Ying, Tian attempts to build a new moral framework based on sincerity and trust.

Besides the maneuver between historicity and contemporaneity, Tian also straddles between China and the West in this version of *The Orphan of Zhao* through the signature syncretism that she draws from Chinese traditional theatre and the performance vocabularies associated with Artaud and Bausch. Dominated by large planes of red and black, the stage bears the imprint of Tian's collaborator Luo Jiangtao, a German-trained scenic designer (Stuttgart; Karlsruhe) whose austere geometry and high-contrast palette shape the production's expressionist look. An enlarged, vein-like motif – adapted from a fragment of a painting by the Chinese-French artist Zao Wou-Ki – runs across the set, while concealed mechanics enable swift transitions: interlinked black wooden panels flip open and shut to create fluid entrances and exits. The production also mobilizes the sign system of traditional Chinese theatre; for example, soldiers running around the stage holding a sword in one hand and a red bundle in the other symbolize the massacre scene in Tian's production. These soldiers function similarly to the *longtao* in traditional theatre, serving as supernumeraries (Yu 2005: 146–7).

In Tian's early works, beginning with *The Field of Life and Death* (1999), the physical language is strikingly prominent, often surpassing the spoken text. In the *Stage Workbook* for *The Orphan of Zhao*, Tian discusses the physicality of the actors. She asserts that "drama is the performing art of living people … it unfolds the story through the actions and collisions of living beings," thereby creating a resonance with the audience. She once again invokes Artaud's *Theatre of Cruelty*, expressing her dislike for plays where characters merely stand and speak. Instead, she yearns for "heat" on stage – an energy that emanates from the actors' lines, their mental states, and their physical movements (Tian 2010b: 142–4). The stage directions in *The Orphan of Zhao* reflect this philosophy: "Tu'an Gu grabs Cheng Ying; the torso remains still, muscles tense, conveying tension; or pause, with a sculptural quality, this group resembles black bas-reliefs" (Tian 2010b: 126).

The actors are instructed to fully utilize their bodies and strength, sometimes delivering exaggerated shouts and broad physical movements. In keeping with the sculptural quality of the production, they are also directed to speak slowly, word by word, stretching the pauses between each. The powerful stage imagery culminates at the play's conclusion, where Tian dramatically juxtaposes two key scenes: one from sixteen years earlier, in which Cheng Ying gives up his child to replace the orphan, and his wife subsequently commits suicide; the other from the present, in which the orphan's true identity is revealed. In these final moments, the four characters – Tu'an Gu, Cheng Ying, his wife, and the orphan – suffer in extreme fear and despair, crying uncontrollably, their voices hoarse, as the atmosphere builds to an intense emotional peak.

The Orphan of Zhao represents one of Tian's most unrestrained uses of physical language, a freedom that reflects the institutional support she received, enabling her to experiment and push the boundaries of theatrical expression.

3.2 Adapting Lao She's *The Yellow Storm*: Turning a Main Melody Play into a Bestseller

On October 30, 2010, Tian Qinxin's adaptation of *The Yellow Storm*, written by the renowned modern Chinese author Lao She (1899–1966), premiered at the

National Sun Yat-sen Memorial Hall in Taipei, Taiwan, marking the beginning of its extraordinary success in both box office and critical acclaim. Within a year, the play was performed over eighty times in nineteen major cities across China, generating box office revenues exceeding twenty million RMB (approximately 2.7 million USD). Reports indicated its remarkable popularity, with nearly every performance sold out and audiences queuing overnight for tickets. In the city of Tianjin, the overwhelming demand resulted in large crowds swarming the theatre, necessitating police intervention to maintain order and causing a temporary five-minute pause in the performance. This intense public interest reflects the play's profound resonance with audiences nationwide (Liu 2011: 1). Over the past fourteen years, *The Yellow Storm* has toured more than thirty cities in China, celebrating its 330th performance in December 2023 at its home venue, the NTC in Beijing.

When Tian began this project, she was already an established director at the NTC, at the age of 41, with considerable experience in generating box office success and managing promotional campaigns, alongside her producer Li Dong, following her productions of *The Red Rose, The White Rose* (2007), and *Ming* (2008). One of her key strategies for *The Yellow Storm* was all-star casting. The cast for the 2010 Taipei premiere featured nine film stars, including celebrated award-winners Huang Lei and Qin Hailu. However, the main attraction for the general public lay in the strong nationalist sentiments and emotional depth evoked by Lao She's work, and Tian's masterful adaptation of it for the stage.

Lao She, born Shu Qingchun in Beijing, was a celebrated Chinese novelist and playwright of Manchu descent, renowned for his vivid portrayal of everyday life and his compassionate social critique, particularly focused on Beijing. In an interview, Tian discussed her personal connection to the work. The original author, Lao She, was of Manchu ethnicity and a relative of Tian's. Both hail from Beijing and share a deep love for the city. Tian had long aspired to create a grand production that captures the distinct cultural essence of Beijing. Her goal was to bring Lao She's "epic of the ordinary people" to the stage, preserving the rich local flavour of the original text (Tang and Mu 2011: 23).

Lao She's works, including *Rickshaw Boy* and *Teahouse*, are notable for their blend of humor, satire, and keen observation of human nature. Lao She was also a pioneer in integrating modern vernacular Chinese into literary forms, making his writing accessible to a wider audience. One of his major works, *The Yellow Storm*, also known as *Four Generations Under One Roof*, was written during the Second Sino-Japanese War (1937–1945, known in China as the War of Resistance against Japanese Aggression), while Lao She resided in Chongqing, the wartime capital. The novel, consisting of approximately 850,000 words, is a trilogy composed of three parts: "Bewilderment," "Living in Shame," and "Famine." Each part provides a vivid depiction of life in Beijing under Japanese occupation, focusing on the experiences of four generations within a single household. "Bewilderment" addresses the initial shock of the invasion and the resulting disorientation. "Living in Shame" examines the compromises and moral conflicts under occupation, while "Famine" portrays the devastation of the human condition under extreme deprivation. Through these narratives, Lao She presents a comprehensive picture of wartime survival, community dynamics, and the human spirit in crisis. The novel serves as both a tribute to the resilience of ordinary Chinese citizens and a critique of those who collaborated with the occupying forces. For Tian, *The Yellow Storm* offered precisely the kind of vast, people-centered narrative she envisioned staging: one that conveyed the collective trauma of war while foregrounding the texture of everyday life in Beijing.

Critics such as David D. W. Wang have noted the novel's overtly patriotic tone, pointing out that "even the trilogy *Four Generations*, acclaimed for its lyrical yearning for traditional life and its deep pathos over China's fate, can hardly avoid didactic passages and sentimental interpolations" (Wang 1989: 199). Nevertheless, the work has been recognized as one of the most significant achievements in modern Chinese literature (Chou 2016: 162). The novel was adapted into a television series in 1985 and 2009, further cementing its popularity. Tian's decision to adapt it for the stage not only reaffirms its cultural importance but also channels Lao She's literary heritage through the medium of theatre, reclaiming Beijing's historical and emotional landscape for contemporary audiences.

Tian's adaptation, heavily funded with a budget of ten million RMB, was coproduced by the NTC, Beijing Performance Co. Ltd., Xicheng District Government of Beijing, Beijing Youth Culture Art Company, and Beijing Children's Theatre Joint Stock Company, with promotion managed by Beijing Julong Cultural Company (Mei 2011: 12). This collaboration exemplified the combined efforts of government and performance institutions to capitalize on the market potential of the "main melody" genre. Originally a musical term, "main melody" (*zhuxuanlü*) was appropriated in the late 1980s as state cultural policy to promote works with didactic intent (Yu 2013: 170). Since then, "main melody" themes have proliferated in films, novels, TV dramas, and stage plays, often featuring patriotic stories from both ancient and modern China.

While some main melody works have achieved notable success in both the domestic market and artistic quality, they have also faced criticism. A central concern raised by critics is that main melody themes often take precedence over artistic form. For instance, Chen Wenyong, a scholar at Henan Normal University, argued that many main melody plays from the 1990s are rendered inauthentic by their overly idealized characters, and that their propagandistic narratives undermine artistic merit (Chen 2013: 96).

Tian, however, has managed to stage main melody plays that avoid overt propaganda while maintaining high artistic standards. Her deep engagement with Chinese culture and history allows her to present these themes with nuance and sensitivity, resonating with audiences beyond didactic messaging.[16]

Hutcheon describes the adaptation of lengthy novels as "a surgical art," as it requires the adapter to engage in a process of subtraction or contraction that inevitably results in some loss of complexity. While most reviewers view this reduction negatively, Hutcheon argues that when plots are condensed and concentrated, they can sometimes become more powerful (Hutcheon 2006: 36). This is especially true when transforming a lengthy novel for the stage. Lao She's original work portrays the lives of one hundred and thirty characters from seventeen families during a turbulent period in history. In her adaptation, Tian restructures the novel's expansive trilogy as a three-act play, streamlining the cast by eliminating numerous characters and concentrating the narrative on three key families – the Qi, Guan, and Qian families. Each act compresses the events, intensifying the central conflicts. This structural approach not only accentuates the main storyline but also creates a cohesive and compelling narrative framework. The progression of time across the acts, from summer to autumn and winter, mirrors the novel's tripartite structure, with the changing seasons and environments symbolically reflecting the rapid passage of history. Tian also added a *shuoshu ren* (storyteller character), who, as both an observer and narrator, connects the three acts of the play, providing a summarized depiction of the lives and shifting fortunes of the characters. Each time the storyteller appears, he breaks the "fourth wall" between the stage and the audience. Moreover, he often engages in spontaneous dialogue with the audience, adding an element of improvisation to the performance.

Adapting a full-length novel into a three-hour play requires not only streamlining the plot and characters but also addressing how the narrative space is handled. Lao She sets the novel's primary location in *Xiaoyangjuan Hutong* (Little Sheepcote Alley), a narrow alley surrounded by residential buildings in Beijing. The challenge lies in how to present the hutong on stage, as well as how to represent the spaces within the hutong, three families, and the courtyards. The stage design was created by Xue Dianjie, who had previously collaborated with Tian on *The Field of Life and Death* (Tang and Mu 2011: 24–5). The design

---

[16] After being appointed Chief Director and later head of the NTC, Tian presided over a series of large-scale *main-melody* commissions that consolidated her public role as a teller of "China's stories."

featured a movable stage, with a courtyard that could be physically pushed. At the center of the stage was the exit of the hutong; to the left was the Qi family, while the Guan and Qian families were located to the right, with a small gate leading to a courtyard near the Qian family. In the middle of the stage was an open space, the main area where most of the characters' actions took place. Of the three households, the Qian family's front gate was positioned center stage, directly facing the audience, with the interior of the courtyard left unseen. The Qian family's actions, including Mr Qian's arrest and Qian Mengshi's funeral, were staged in this open area. The courtyards of the Qi and Guan families, positioned on either side, were moveable; during scenes involving these families, the actors themselves would push open the courtyard walls, transforming the small space into either the Qi or Guan courtyards, thereby expanding the spatial possibilities. Once the scene was finished, the actors would push the walls offstage. This stage design brought all three families into view on one stage. Whereas in the real hutong, families would have their doors firmly shut, this design allowed the audience to glimpse into their lives.

Although the fixed setting was the *hutong*, many events that took place outside the alley also needed representation. When the story moved beyond the alley, men pedaling tricycles acted as live revolving stages with the characters performing in a distanced manner, conveying what they saw and did. For example, in the first act, Guan Xiaohuo's "running for office in troubled times" is depicted; in the second act, the Tiananmen Square gathering; and in the third, the Nanhai Incident. This approach extends the stage's spatial capacity. The use of pedal tricycles to transition between scenes is perhaps the most abstract element in this otherwise realist drama. Tian describes her adaptation, which she cowrote and directed, as "new realism," a form of neo-realism (Chou 2016: 163).

Critics observed that this adaptation was less radical and experimental than Tian's earlier works, displaying a more measured tone. Katherine Hui-Ling Chou raises the question of whether Tian followed certain "guidelines" to ensure that the production aligned with mainstream "orthodox drama" (*zhengju*), thus increasing its potential for commercial success (Chou 2016: 165). Tian acknowledged that this shift is related to her mature age and mindset (Tang and Mu 2011: 27). It had been eleven years since her adaptation of *The Field of Life and Death*, a period that also witnessed the commercialization of Chinese theatre. From *The Field of Life and Death* to *The Yellow Storm*, Tian undoubtedly mastered techniques more aligned with mainstream aesthetics, which also had greater box-office appeal. While both works address the theme of resistance against Japanese occupation, *The Field of Life and Death* foregrounds issues of gender and nationalism, whereas *The Yellow Storm* highlights a more traditional nationalist ideal – the allegorical narrative of the unity between home and nation.

Professor Kong Qingdong of Peking University mentioned that during his discussion with Tian about *The Yellow Storm*, he posed these questions: if Lao She wanted to write a novel about the eight years of Peking's occupation by the Japanese, why did he choose the title *Four Generations under One Roof*? Is there a connection between this well-known Chinese concept of "four generations under one roof" and the "eight-year War of Resistance?" What is the nature of that connection? Kong believes that Lao She viewed the Chinese philosophy as fundamentally a "getting by" philosophy, with *Four Generations under One Roof* representing the pinnacle of this way of life, especially the Qis' endeavor to survive the Sino-Japanese War (1937–1945) and to live the Confucian ideal of "four generations sharing the same roof." According to Kong, both the strengths and weaknesses of the Chinese nation stem from this concept of "getting by." The single-minded pursuit of "four generations under one roof" led to the negligence of other important matters, rendering the country vulnerable to invasion and its people susceptible to enslavement. Yet, this same pursuit also enabled the people to rise up so that the nation could achieve liberation (Kong 2011: 34). In this sense, Lao She merges the history of the War of Resistance and the history of ordinary people's daily life, which sees the larger picture through the smaller. He writes like an anthropologist about the city's seasonal features, customs, rituals, and the people's emotions and interactions. The serene, beautifully remembered homeland, filled with warmth and humanity, stands in stark contrast to the harsh reality of Japanese invasion and oppression, thereby further evoking a deep sense of empathy and resonance in the reader (Kong 2011: 34).

According to Kong, Tian has captured all these essential elements in her adaptation. Like Lao She did with words, she reconstructs an ethnographic picture of old Beijing on stage (Kong 2011: 34). As Tian herself summarises, the theme of the stage adaptation of *The Yellow Storm* is the resilience of ordinary Chinese people trying to survive in chaotic times (Tang and Mu 2011: 26). It is precisely this interplay of individual and national emotions, the spatial setting of old Beijing's hutongs, the Beijing dialect, and imagery interwoven with anti-Japanese nationalism that enabled this mainstream play to achieve great box office success. The production also resonated with audiences in Taiwan. *The Yellow Storm* marked the first time that a spoken drama from the mainland premiered in Taiwan. Although Chou suggests that "the decision to open the show in Taipei was probably more commercial than political" (Chou 2016:160), the deepening of historical and cultural ties across the Taiwan Strait has always remained a political aim. According to a report by the Ministry of Culture and Tourism, the performances in Taipei resonated deeply with audiences on both sides of the Taiwan Strait, rekindling a shared cultural heritage and national sentiment (Yi 2011). Kong argues that Taiwan's cultural community harbors a "spatial imagination" of Beijing's culture. Their anticipation of this play was a desire to "enter another space that is both unfamiliar and familiar" to complete a temporal heritage continuity and fulfill their own "self-sufficient national consciousness" (Kong 2011: 34).

The Yellow Storm shows how Tian turned an epic, overtly patriotic novel into an audience-grabbing "new realism." The production mobilized main-melody affect while avoiding crude propaganda through local detail, ethical shading, and a calibrated tone. Its cross-Strait premiere and sustained national run signal not only commercial power but also the reactivation of shared cultural memory. Again, this successful adaptation crystallizes Tian's method: institutional savvy plus adaptive craft yielding mass appeal and cultural resonance.

3.3 Adapting Shakespeare: Tian's Playful Theatricals in *Ming*

In 2008, the NTC launched its international theatre season, *Shakespeare Forever*, with the premiere of Tian Qinxin's Chinese adaptation of *King Lear*, retitled *Ming*. The production premiered on October 10 at the National Centre for the Performing Arts in Beijing as the festival's opening performance. Producer Li Dong's retitling and re-siting were a deliberate brand strategy: the title *Ming* was chosen to build on the mass readership of Dangnian Mingyue (Shi Yue)'s bestselling series *Stories about the Ming Dynasty*, aligning the production with a recognized IP and widening the audience beyond Shakespeare specialists (Wang 2019: 161). To consolidate the link, Tian invited Shi Yue to write the script, allowing the show to be presented and marketed within a familiar historical frame. Commercially, relocating the action to the Ming dynasty (1368–1644) reduced cultural distance for domestic audiences, matched prevailing market taste for Ming-themed narratives, and supplied clear hooks for publicity, partnerships, and ticket sales. In this reimagining, Lear becomes Zhu Yuanzhang (1328–1398), the founding emperor of Ming, and the three daughters become three sons; beyond this premise, the production diverges substantially from Shakespeare's play in plot, themes, and theatrical language.

Ming is replete with parodic impulses and meta-theatrical elements, including plays-within-the-play and role-playing. The ageing Emperor Zhu, preparing to abdicate, introduces Shakespeare's script and, accompanied by his three sons, leads a reading of the play. As they proceed, they not only perform but also comment on the action:

Emperor: . . . Following the script of *King Lear*, let us perform a play-within-the-play. Now, speak of your love for your father.

Eldest Prince: I am the eldest, so I shall begin. Father, I love you, I love you most.

Eunuch: You are playing the eldest daughter.
[The eunuch hands a flower to the eldest son.]

Eldest Prince: Don't block me from acting! I am the eldest daughter now. This kind of love cannot be expressed in words. Father, I love you. This love surpasses everything precious and rare in the world. Father, I love you so much . . . . . .

Emperor: And my third son? Speak.

Third Prince: Father, I can only give you half of my love, for I am to marry. The other half must be given to my husband. This foreign daughter is truly frank – doesn't she fear punishment? (Tian 2010b: 8)

Emperor: I say, he does not understand the ways of our Great Ming . . . The Great Ming, vast and fertile, with its towering mountains, expansive plains, rivers, lakes, and seas – everyone desires the best land. The city is divided – who will take the outskirts? The plains are divided – who will take the mountains? Those places with rivers, lakes, and seas – who will take the interior? (Tian 2010b: 10)

This scene uses the framework of Shakespeare's *King Lear* to reflect on the nature of feudal power struggles in China. Unlike Lear's kingdom, which can be divided among his daughters, the Chinese empire is indivisible. It can only have one ruler. Thus, the central issue here is the identification of a successor. The selection of an emperor in China is a process of great complexity, fraught with intense conflict. This is a theme frequently depicted in contemporary Chinese palace dramas. In *Ming*, the old emperor intentionally provokes rivalry among his sons, observing quietly from a distance as they battle for supremacy. He ultimately chooses the son who prevails in the struggle for power to inherit the throne. This approach contrasts with King Lear, whose inability to navigate the intersection of familial ethics and political reality blinds him to the consequences of his decision. Lear loses both his kingdom and his beloved daughter Cordelia. In contrast, the emperor in *Ming* is calculating, coldly watching the sons' self-destructive quarrels, controlling the outcome of their struggle with secretive manipulation (Wang 2019: 161).

This approach clearly subverts the tragic theme of *King Lear*, transforming it into a cold and ruthless variant of *Game of Thrones*:

Third Prince: Was all of this your design?

Emperor: It was.

Third Prince: Has everything I've done until now been orchestrated by you?

Emperor: Come on—let's perform the ending of the play-within-the-play based on King Lear, and tell us about your love for your father.

Everyone: Watch the play. Watch the play.

Third Prince: You've controlled everything!

Emperor: Yes, I have.

...

Third Prince: We brothers murdering each other, and you remain indifferent . . . your own flesh and blood, yet you stand by as they die.

Emperor: I choose not to intervene. (Tian 2010b: 59)

Tian explains that the creation of *Ming* was an arduous process, as it was saturated with power struggles and intrigue, themes she admitted she was not naturally adept at expressing (Tian 2010b: 12). Yet these very themes resonate strongly with Chinese audiences, who have long been captivated by depictions of palace politics and the machinations of power in literature, opera, and popular media. In *Ming*, this "Game of Thrones" motif is further underscored by the stage design, which evokes a nihilistic sense of the transient and hollow nature of power. The set design, created by installation artist Xia Xiaowan (1959–), features a vast Chinese landscape painting as the backdrop. In both the opening and closing scenes, sixteen Ming emperors, draped in dragon robes, appear, symbolizing the enduring continuity of the empire and implying that all others are mere transient visitors. In this regard, *Ming* functions as a less deferential and arguably more critical parody of Shakespeare's classic, subverting its original themes.

In addition to the thematic shift, the most significant subversion in Tian's adaptation lies in her theatrical presentation, which draws heavily on the conventions of Chinese traditional theatre. She fully embraces the concept of playful theatrics discussed earlier in this work. In *Tian Qinxin's Dramas Script*, she elaborates on her bold experiment with *Ming*:

> I now favour a more open approach to theatre; I no longer appreciate the constraints of rigid structures. In this production, the performance shifts in and out; the actors are free to drink tea on stage, and anyone can step forward to perform when needed. Sometimes, they step out of character to speak as actors. In Chinese theatre, particularly during stage inspections, the audience

understands exactly what is occurring. Chinese theatre is based on assumptions; the audience does not take everything literally. The actors themselves don't perform with absolute seriousness; they know what the audience expects and offer an opportunistic performance. On stage, the actors must remain alert and perceptive. I am trying to restore this tradition (Tian 2010b: 45).

Here, Tian is clearly critiquing the rigidity of canonical Shakespeare productions on the Chinese stage. She seeks to subvert what she perceives as a Westernized approach, instead bringing *Ming* back to the more relaxed, flexible atmosphere of traditional Chinese theatre. For instance, at the opening, all sixteen actors, dressed in imperial robes, march to the front of the stage to greet the audience with a quintessential *xiqu* performance idiom:

Everyone: Upstairs.
[The entire cast bows to the audience]
Please set your phones to vibrate.
[The entire cast bows]
If you haven't yet had dinner,
[The entire cast bows]
...
Thank you for listening without growing bored.
[The entire cast bows] (Tian 2010b: 3) (see Figure 6).

Following the exposition, the actors change costumes, shedding their imperial robes and draping them over mannequins at the back of the stage. They then step into their roles but frequently break character to make comments that aim to amuse the audience. For example, the actor portraying the old emperor uses

Figure 6 Opening scene from *Ming*. Photo taken by the author during the National Theatre of China's year-end production at the Poly Theatre, Beijing, December 10, 2008.

a distancing technique to reflect on the role: "This job is incredibly demanding; every morning, you must wake up early, like attending an early class. The difference is that everyone else has a teacher, but the emperor's early class lasts a lifetime." In *Ming*, the actors swiftly change costumes on stage and transition into the play-within-the-play, *King Lear*, where the roles become multilayered: the emperor and King Lear; the eldest son and eldest daughter; the second son and second daughter; the third son and third daughter. In this fluidity, the actors constantly leap in and out of various identities.

In fact, Tian's postmodern adaptation and parody of Shakespeare, incorporating elements distinctive of *xiqu* performance, is part of a broader trend. In *Chinese Shakespeares: Two Centuries of Cultural Exchange* (2009), Alexander C. Y. Huang traces a century of Chinese engagements with Shakespeare and observes that by the 1990s, "Shakespeare" had become both a familiar text and a highly marketable cultural commodity for Chinese theatre audiences. Some Shakespearean plays had become so ingrained in the cultural landscape that directors began to exploit this presumed familiarity to create innovative works or new performance styles. Huang observes:

> This familiarity with Shakespeare, coupled with a diversification of interpretive perspectives, made it possible for new works that were no longer simply focused on retelling Shakespeare's stories. The question of "China," however, had been the dominant concern for *xiqu* (Chinese opera) and *huaju* (modern Chinese drama) theatres for so long that some artists began to avoid constructing a core narrative centered on Chinese politics and aesthetics. (Huang 2009: 199)

Huang goes on to highlight how, from the 1990s to the new millennium, theatre directors produced increasingly "localised" interpretations of Shakespeare, infused with a distinctly personal engagement. These new forms of performance included parody or scripted "improvisation," such as Lee Kuo-hsiu's *Shamlet* (1992), Stan Lai's *Lear and the Thirty-seven-fold Practice of a Bodhisattva* (2000), fragmented "remixes" of Shakespeare, like the Shakespeare's Wild Sisters Company's *Crazy Scenes* (2002), based on scenes of madness in *Hamlet*, *Macbeth*, *King Lear*, and *Othello*; as well as solo performances such as Tian Mansha's *Lady Macbeth* (2001). Among these adaptations, Wu Hsingkuo's *Lear Is Here* (2001) stood out, a collage based on *King Lear* in which Wu restructures the play through a postmodern lens that challenges the *jingju* (Peking opera) aesthetic of abstraction (Huang 2009: 200).

Tian's adaptation of *King Lear* is even more drastic. She seeks to reconfigure the tragedy into a more relaxed, entertaining form, drawing on traditional

Chinese theatrical conventions to introduce a sense of ease and pleasure. As she explains:

> I aim to restore a specific spirit of entertainment intrinsic to Chinese theatre. But what exactly defines Chinese performance? This is something we can ponder – stepping in and out of roles, donning costumes, adopting a casual, "improvised" approach to acting. This style offers the audience both a visual and auditory comfort. After a long day's work, watching a play should be a source of genuine pleasure ... Pleasure, after all, is a form of spiritual nourishment ... (Tian 2010b: 43)

In this instance, Tian seems to be challenging the model of Chinese *huaju* (spoken theatre) that has prevailed since the May Fourth Movement at the beginning of the twentieth century. Not only has *huaju* prioritized seriousness and decorum, but it has often done so at the cost of relaxation and ease. This is largely a result of *huaju*'s Western influences, particularly its alignment with nineteenth-century Western realist theatre (Huang 2009: 170). Tian likely recognized that the relaxed, entertaining qualities characteristic of traditional Chinese opera would better resonate with contemporary audiences – a realization that also reflects commercial considerations. This playful theatricality appears as a defining feature in many of her commercially driven adaptations, with *Ming* serving as an early example. It reappears in her subsequent works, such as *Red Rose, White Rose* (2010), *Green Snake* (2013), and her adaptation of *Romeo and Juliet* (2014).

Of course, one may wonder whether Tian's Chinese-inflected playful theatricals really work. *Ming* is characterized by a continuous oscillation, with actors frequently stepping in and out of roles in a manner reminiscent of comic interludes, aimed at lightening the atmosphere. In her pursuit of comedic effect, Tian invited Chinese folk artists – particularly practitioners of lowbrow art forms like *Er Ren Zhuan* and *Xiang Sheng* (cross-talk) – to mentor the actors. This approach became one of the most prominent methods used to "amuse the audience" in *Ming*. However, due to its repetitive nature, few viewers were able to sustain their amusement throughout the entire play. Critics argue that the intended lightness did not materialize; rather than creating relaxation, the play's innovative performance style appeared flawed, with the actors' exertions leaving the audience more fatigued than at ease. The dynamic between performer and spectator failed to produce the intended enjoyment; instead, it resulted in a fragmented narrative that left the audience bewildered. The frequent shifts in character weakened the continuity of the plot, and when actors stepped out of their roles, they became part of the backdrop, with as many as seven or eight actors sitting offstage, watching the performance unfold. The intention was to create an atmosphere of freedom, but excessive freedom led to confusion in both the storyline and the stage direction, thereby obscuring the play's themes (Wang 2019: 162). Tian herself candidly acknowledged that the experiment was not entirely successful. In *Tian's Drama Script*, she reflects:

> In this play, I aimed to explore a different performance approach. I wanted to revive a form of Chinese theatre that had been lost. Restoration, searching for, and re-enacting are challenging tasks; it's an undertaking. Perhaps what we've created is still a work-in-progress, but I have no regrets. I'm deeply grateful to the actors for their willingness to take on such a difficult performance. It was incredibly challenging, but also immensely fulfilling. Because I pushed boundaries (Tian 2010b: 20).

Nonetheless, Tian repeated this approach in her next Shakespeare adaptation – *Romeo and Juliet* for the forty-second Hong Kong Arts Festival in 2014. The play is likewise completely reimagined as a contemporary narrative with modern characters: two feuding families, a group of punk-styled youths, a cross-dressing nurse, and a rock-singing priest. This reconfiguration imbues the adaptation with a distinctly playful quality, which resonates with the dramatic sensibilities and viewing expectations of younger audiences, aligning with their tastes and perspectives. In this regard, Tian's adaptations of Shakespeare are not intercultural exchanges but rather acts of localization. By discarding the original story and incorporating extensive local elements, she reframes the play for her vision of "Chinese theatre." However, this approach faces a significant challenge: The Western classics themselves have been deconstructed and reinterpreted so frequently that the meanings they once carried have been all but exhausted. Consequently, many adaptations, including Tian's, risk becoming little more than formal experiments in stagecraft, at times prioritizing style over substance. This often results in adaptations that fall short of fostering meaningful cross-cultural dialogue, instead becoming exercises in surface-level theatrics that fail to generate substantive intercultural exchange (Fan 2015: 81).

In sum, *Ming* epitomizes Tian and Li's market-savvy localization of Shakespeare: a strategic rebrand, a shift to the Ming court, and a playful *xiqu*-inflected dramaturgy that courts mainstream audiences. Yet it also exposes the limit of that approach.

Conclusion

Tian Qinxin's career has been shaped by the great changes that China's *huaju* (spoken drama) circle has undergone in the new millennium. Two other prominent directors, Meng Jinghui and Yu Rongjun, work both inside and outside the establishment. In contrast, Tian is more firmly entrenched inside the establishment, not least through her longstanding affiliation with the NTC, as both a director and (as of 2020) its head. Over the years, Tian has achieved what Katherine Hui-Ling Chou calls "a utopian balance between marketing strategy, artistic ambition, and state policy" (Chou 2016: 162). Chou's point is apt considering how skillfully Tian has maneuvered through various and sometimes difficult subjects and materials.

In a field that has historically constrained women in China, Tian's sustained success invites exploration: How, in practice, has she achieved this "utopian balance"? Her success rests on a powerful synthesis of artistic instinct, adaptability in both her own roles and her productions, and institutional acumen. A deep fascination with theatre shapes her approach to gender performance and adaptation. For Tian, gender shifts are not merely superficial gestures but strategies that support her own authority as a director while also shaping her theatrical practice, where role-playing and identity fluidity become central to the expansion of performative possibilities on stage. Timely institutional support has provided her with the resources and freedom to experiment within, and at times to extend, prevailing norms. As a result, her main-melody works carry grandeur and ethical seriousness, while her commercial productions embrace a spirit of playfulness. From *The Field of Life and Death* (1999) to *Green Snake* (2013), she has consistently moved between seriousness and play, weaving together Western theatrical vocabularies with the textures of Chinese stage traditions.

Her adaptations of female narratives are especially revealing. Rather than simply "updating" protagonists, she repositions them within new ethical and affective coordinates: The Orphan of Zhao follows the story of Zhuangji in an ancient text but gives her complexity; *Green Snake* elevates female desire from subtext to a motor of action; Red Rose, White Rose interrogates split selves and the social scripts of love. In *Ming*, cross-dressing functions as a means to denaturalize gendered authority and expose performance as a system of codes. Tian's position as a woman directing within – and ultimately leading – national institutions complicates any simple feminist reading; precisely from this positionality, she stages the friction between emancipation and normativity, private emotion and public narrative. Her navigation between seriousness and play is, in this sense, also a negotiation between female subjectivity and mainstream frameworks.

Dramaturgically, Tian specializes in distilling voluminous or structurally diffuse sources into performable scripts, then animating them with *xiqu*-inflected "playful theatrics": meta-theatrical self-address, stepping in and out of role, visible costume shifts, and comic relief drawn from folk modes. She counterbalances these with a physically charged score – sculptural pauses, bas-relief groupings, and an expressionist palette – that can pivot from intimacy to pageant. The result is a recognizable Tian dialect: audience-forward and market-savvy yet capable of ethical argument, voiced either in the rhetoric of contemporary values or through the home-and-nation allegory characteristic of main-melody work.

Read together, Tian's career offers a woman theatre-maker's blueprint for working from within the state system in a market age: Adapt boldly, entertain openly, argue ethically. As a woman who leads a national institution, she shows how female authorship can convert institutional capital into artistic latitude – yet her practice also clarifies the limits of that bargain. The same devices that court broad audiences – compression, meta-theatre, playful codes – may, when overused, thin the fabric of narrative or soften tragic pressure; at their best, they keep classical materials legible while opening space for female subjectivity, desire, and ethical agency. This double movement – between old and new, authority and autonomy, solemnity and play – defines Tian's distinctive contribution and sketches the possibilities for future women theatre-makers at the intersection of artistry, commerce, and the state.

References

Allen, Joseph R. 1996. "Dressing and Undressing the Chinese Woman Warrior." *Positions* 4.2: 343–79.

Artaud, Antonine. 1958. *The Theatre and Its Double*. Trans. Mary Caroline Richards. New York: Grove Press, Inc.

Barlow, Tani E. 2004. *The Question of Women in Chinese Feminism*. Durham: Duke University Press.

Butler, Judith. 1999. *Gender Trouble: Feminism and the Subversion of Identity*. New York: Routledge.

Cao, Shunqing and Shuaidong Zhang. 2020. "Variation in Literature Communication and the Formation of World Literature." *Comparative Literature Studies* 57.3: 475–84.

Chang, Eileen. 2007. *Red Rose, White Rose*. Trans. Karen S. Kingsbury. London: Penguin Books.

Chen, Eva Yin-I. 2009. "Shanghai Baby as a Chinese Chick-Lit: Female Empowerment and Neoliberal Consumerist Agency." *Asian Journal of Women's Studies* 15.1: 54–93.

Chen, Xiaomei. 2002. *Acting the Right Part: Political Theatre and Popular Drama in Contemporary China*. Honolulu: University of Haiwai'i Press.

Chen, Wenyong. 2013. "1990 niandai Zhongguo zhuxuanlu" xiju zhi pipan" [A Critique of China's Main Melody Plays in 1990s]. *Zhongguo xiandai wenxue luncong* (Chinese Modern Literature Forum) 8.2: 95–104.

——— 2023. *Performing the Socialist State: Modern Chinese Theatre and Film Culture*. New York: Columbia University Press.

Chou, Hui-ling. 1997. "Striking Their Own Poses: The History of Cross-Dressing on the Chinese Stage." *The Drama Review* 41.2: 130–52.

Chou, Katherine Hui-Ling. 2016. "Staging a New Venture: Tian Qinxin's The Yellow Storm and the Policy Change on the Huaju Industry in China." In Li Ruru, ed., *Staging China: New Theatres in the Twenty-First Century*. London: Palgrave Macmillan, pp. 159–76.

Chow, Rey. 1999. "Seminal Dispersal, Fecal Retention, and Related Narrative Matters: Eileen Chang's Tale of Roses in the Problematic of Modern Writing." *Differences: A Journal of Feminist Cultural Studies* 11.2: 153–76.

Chun, Tarryn Li-Min. 2019. "Mediated Transgression and Madame White: Technology and the Nonhuman in Contemporary Stagings of a Chinese Folktale." *Theatre Journal* 71.3: 308.

Dai Jinhua. 2007. *Shedu zhizhou: xinshiqi zhongguo nvxing xiezuo yu nxxing wenhua* [Crossing the Ford: Contemporary Chinese Women's Writing and Feminine Culture]. Beijing: Peking University Press.

Dai, Jingting. 2004. "Tian Qinxin: I Use Tradition to Reflect on the Present." *Sina News* (reprinted from *China Newsweek*). https://news.sina.cn/sa/2004-10-25/detail-ikknscsi4617932.d.html, accessed on January 5, 2025.

———. 2015. "Weiwan daxu" [To be Continued by Dai]. www.bilibili.com/video/BV1Zv411u7sF/?spm_id_from=333.337.search-card.all.click&vd_source=2fa55775ed9675d4a142d0163d4c6b22, accessed on June 15, 2024.

Deppman, Hsui-Chuang. 2010. *Adapted for the Screen: The Cultural Politics of Modern Chinese Fiction and Film*. Honolulu: University of Hawai'I Press.

Du Wenei. 2001. "Historicity and Contemporaneity: Adapatation of Yuan Plays in the 1990s." Asian Theatre Journal 18.2: 222–37.

Fan Chunshuang. 2015. "Xijuxingshi zheyi shouduan: Tian Qinxin xiju biaoxian xingshi chutan" [The dramatic form as a means: An exploration of Tian Qinxin's dramatic expression]. *Drama Literature* 391.12: 80–1.

Felski, Rita. 2020. *Hooked: Art and Attachment*. Chicago: The University of Chicago Press.

Ferris, Lesley. 1989. *Acting Women: Images of Women in Theatre*. New York: New York University Press.

Gao, Yin. 2010. "Zhishangzuoxi: wutaigaibian Zhang Ailing" [Drama on paper: The stage adaptation of Eileen Chang]. *Yishu Pinglun* [Art Criticism] 8: 17–21.

Goldblatt, Howard. 2002. "Translator's Introduction." in Xiao Hong, ed., *The Field of Life and Death & Tales of Hulan River*. Trans. Howard Goldblatt. Boston: Chen &Tsui Company.

Howell, Jude. 2014. "Where Are All the Women in China's Political System?" *East Asian Forum*. https://eastasiaforum.org/2014/10/15/where-are-all-the-women-in-chinas-political-system/, accessed on May 17, 2024.

Hsia, Chih-tsing. 1961. *A History of Modern Chinese Fiction*. Bloomington: Indiana University Press.

Hsu, Jen-Hao. 2012. "Queering Chineseness: The Queer Sphere of Feelings in *Farewell My Concubine* and *Green Snake*." *Asian Studies Review* 36.1: 1–17.

Hu, Puzhong. 2010. "Tian Qinxin xiju zhong de Xiaohong yu Zhang Ailing"[Xiao Hong and Zhang Ailing in Tian Qinxin's dramatic works]. *Zhongguo Tushu Pinglun* [China Book Review] 12: 84–8.

Huang, Alexander C. Y. 2009. *Chinese Shakespeares: Two Centuries of Cultural Exchange*. New York: Columbia University Press.

Hutcheon, Linda. 2006. *A Theory of Adaptation*. New York: Routledge.

References

Kaulbach, Barbara M. 1982. "The Woman Warrior in Chinese Opera: An Image of Reality or Fiction?" *Fu Jen Studies: Literature and Linguistics* 15: 69–82.

Kong, Qingdong. 2011. "Lun Sishitongtang de huajugaibian" [On Theatrical Adaptation of *The Yellow Storm*]. *Yishu Pinglun* [Art Criticism] 3: 33–36.

Kristiva, Julia. 1977. *About Chinese Women*. Trans. Anita Barrows. New York: Urizen Books.

Kristiva, Julia. 1977. *About Chinese Women*. Trans. Anita Barrows. New York: Urizen Books.

Li, Ruru. 2016. "Introduction to Part II 'Main Melody': A New Image of Propaganda Theatre." In Li Ruru, ed., *Staging China: New Theatres in the Twenty-First Century*. London: Palgrave Macmillan, pp. 55–60.

Li, Siu Leung. 2003. *Cross-Dressing in Chinese Opera Hong Kong*. Hong Kong: Hong Kong University Press.

Liu, Lydia H. 1995. *Translingual Practice: Literature, National Culture, and Translated Modernity – China, 1900–1937*. Standford: Standford University Press.

Liu, Miao. 2011. "Tian Qinxin: Sishitongtang zuole yiba yingxiong" [Tian Qinxin: Have Become a Hero in *The Yellow Storm*]. *Zhongguo wenhua bao* [Chinese Culture], March 24.

Liu, Siyuan. 2016. "Modern Chinese Theatre." In Liu Siyuan, ed., *Routledge Handbook of Asian Theatre*. New York: Routledge, pp. 311–27.

Liu, Yingying and Wei Yanxing. 2021. "CPPCC Member Tian Qinxin: Telling China's Stories across Boundaries to Illuminate Outstanding Traditional Culture." *People's Daily Online*, http://ent.people.com.cn/n1/2021/0310/c101s2047765.html, accessed on Octobor 2, 2025.

Liu, Yunting. 2019. "Cong Baishezhuan de renxing xiuxing dao Qingshe de rensheng chulu" [From the Path of Cultivation in *The Legend of the White Snake* to the Path of Fulfillment in *Green Snake*]. *Xiju zhijia* [Home Drama] 313.13: 9–10.

Louie, Kam. 2012a. "Introducing Eileen Chang: A Life of Conflicting Cultures in China and America." In Kam Louie, ed., *Eileen Chang:Romancing Languages, Cultures and Genres*. Hong Kong: Hong Kong University of Press, pp. 1–14.

2012b. "Romancing Returnee Men: Masculinity in 'Love in a Fallen City' and 'Red Rose, White Rose'." In Kam Louie, ed., *Eileen Chang: Romancing Languages, Cultures and Genres*. Hong Kong: Hong Kong University of Press, pp. 15–34.

Luo, Liang. 2021. *The Global White Snake*. Ann Arbor: University of Michigan Press.

Ma, Rongrong and Tian Qinxin. 2010. "Xiju chang li de qing yu yi" [Affection and Loyalty in Theatre] *Sanlian shenghuo zhoukan* [Life Week], January 18.

Mackerras, Colin. 2008. "Tradition, Change, and Continuity in Chinese Theatre in the Last Hundred Years: In Commemoration of the Spoken Drama Centenary." *Asian Theatre Journal* 25.1: 1–23.

Mei, Chun. 2011. *The Novel and Theatrical Imagination in Early Modern China*. Leiden: Brill.

Mei, Sheng. 2011. "Qiangqiangliashou quanfangwei dazao wutai jingdian ——Huaju Sishitongtang de shichang yunzuo" [Joining Forces to Create a Stage Classic: The Market Operation of *The Yellow Storm*]. *Xiju wenxue* [Drama Literature] 335.4: 12–13.

Melvin, Sheila. 2008. "A Postmodrtem Revival for China's Acclaimed Author Zhang Ailing." *The New York Times*, www.nytimes.com/2008/01/16/arts/16iht-melvin.1.9252115.html, accessed on May 17, 2024.

Meng, Yue and Dai Jinhua. 2018. *Fuchu lishi dibiao: Xiandai funv wenxue yanjiu* [*Emerging from the Horizon of History: Modern Chinese Women's Literature, 1917–1949*]. Beijing: Peking University Press.

Niu, Chunmei. "Tian Qinxin on the Play *Green Snake*: Received an Invitation from Li Bihua Five Years Ago." *Beijing Daily*, December 13, 2012, http://culture.people.com.cn/n/2012/1213/c22219-19889341.html, accessed on October 2, 2025.

Noble, Jonathan. 2007. "China: Modern Theatre." In Samuel L. Leiter, ed., *Encyclopedia of Asian Theatre, Vol. 1*. Westport, CT: Greenwood Press. pp. 111–7.

Pressely, Nelson. 2014. "National Theatre of China's 'Green Snake' at Kennedy Center Playfully Blends Old and New." The Washington Post, www.washingtonpost.com/entertainment/theater_dance/national-theatre-of-chinas-green-snake-at-kennedy-center-playfully-blends-old-and-new/2014/03/28/63f3f612-b695-11e3-a7c6-70cf2db17781_story.html, accessed on July 23, 2024.

Price, David W. 1990. "The Politics of the Body: Pina Bausch's 'Tanztheater'." *Theatre Journal* 42.3: 322–31.

Rankin, Mary Backus. 1975. "The Emergence of Women at the End of the Ch'ing: The Case of Ch'iu Chin." In Margery Wolf and Roxane Witke eds., *Women in Chinese Society*. Stanford, CA: Stanford University Press, pp. 39–66.

Shui, Jing. "*Green Snake: An International Presentation of a Traditional Story*." *China Art News*, April 24, 2013, www.cflac.org.cn/ys/xwy/201304/t20130424_185096.html, accessed on Octobor 2, 2025.

Song, Yu. 2016. "Institutionalising Rural Women's Political Participation in China: Reserved Seats Election for Women." *Asian Women*, 32.3: 77–99.

"Tanban Sishitongtang pailian chang, juli 'mingxing ban' yanchu jin sheng yitian" [Behind-the-Scenes at the all-star Cast Rehearsal of *The Yellow Storm*: Only One Day until the Premier]. 2023. National Theatre of China. https://mp.weixin.qq.com/s?__biz=MjM5NTgwMjI5NQ==&mid=2652558094&idx=1&sn=4f1d65198dad5ea9471f818204fed9aa&chksm=bd1c8ed68a6b07c0770eabf49e1d6e53618f8d27035902508f124cb2f701afafa04dbf137b33&scene=27, accessed November 13, 2024.

Tang, Ling and Mu Sen. 2011. "Shendu fangtan: huaju Sishitongtang bianju daoyan Tian Qinxin" [In Conversation with Tian Qinxin: Writer and Director of *The Yellow Storm*]. *Yishu Pinlun* [Art Criticism] 3: 23–7.

Tang, Ling and Mu Sen. 2011. "Shendu fangtan: Huaju Sishitongtang bianju daoyan Tian Qinxin" [In conversation with Tian Qinxin: writer and director of *The Yellow Storm*]. *Yishu Pinlun* [Art Criticism] 3: 23–27.

Tharu, Susie J. 1984. *The Sense of Performance: Post-Artaud Theatre*. Atlantic Highlands: Humanities Press.

Tian, Chuan and Tian Qinxin. 2022. "S Face mingren mianduimian: Duihua Tian Qinxin" [S Face Celebrities Face-to-Face: A Conversation with Tian Qinxin]. Phoenix Television. https://baijiahao.baidu.com/s?id=1745840945412336931&wfr=spider&for=pc, accessed on November 17, 2024.

Tian, Qinxin. 2003. *Wo zuo xi yinwei wo beishang* [I Write Play for I Am Sad]. Beijing: The Witers' Publishing House.

 2010a. *Tian Qinxin de xijuchang* [Tian Qinxin's Drama Field]. Beijing: Peking University Press.

 2010b. *Tian Qinxin de xijuben* [Tian Qinxin's Drama Script]. Beijing: Peking University Press.

 2019. "Tian Qinxin tan Xiao Hong" [Tian Qinxin Talking about Xiao Hong]. Douban. www.douban.com/note/704552538/?_i=4483020bb0iTZ_, accessed on July 19, 2024.

Tian, Qinxin and An ying. 2013. "Qingshe" [Green Snake]. *Xin juben* [New Drama] 178.4: 9–57.

Tian, Qinxin, Wan Shurong, and Zhu yuning. 2009. "Tian Qinxin daoyan tan huaju gaibian" [Director Tian Qinxin Talking about Adaptation in Theatre]. *Xiyuan* [Forum of Arts] 6: 7.

Tian, Qinxin and Wei Lixin, 2003. "Zai xiju mianqian geren shi miaoxiao de" [Individuals are Insignificant in the Face of Drama]. In Wei Lixin, ed., *Zuo xi: xijuren shuo* [*Making Theatre: What Theater People Say*]. Beijing: Culture and Arts Press. pp. 27–43.

Wang, David D. W. 1989. "Lao She's Wartime Fiction." *Modern Chinese Literature*, 5.2: 197–218.
Wang, Xijin. 2019. "Huifu zhongguo chuantong jingshen de yici changshi:ping gaibian Shashibiya Lierwang de huaju Ming" [An Effort to Restore the Traditional Chinese Spirits: Reviewing *Ming*, a Chinese Adaptation of Shakespeare's *King Lear*]. *Mingri fengshang* [The Fashion of Tomorrow] 24: 161–2.
Wang, Yan, Ding Chao and Hu Puzhong. et al. 2010. "Yu Tian Qinxin daoyan duitan huaju shinian" [A Decade of Theatre: A Conversation with Director Tian Qinxin]. *Yishu Pinglun* [Art Criticism] 8: 26–32.
Wang, Kai. 2011. "Tian Qinxin zai pailianchang: shanglu de guer" [Tian Qinxin on Stage: An Orphan on the Road]. *Sanlian shenghuo zhoukan* [Life Week], September 5.
Wen, Rumin. 2004. "Jin ershi nian Zhang Ailing zai dalu de jieshou shi" [The Reception of Eileen Chang's Work in Mainland China in the Last Two Decades]. In Liu Shaoming, Liang Bingjun and Xu Zidong et al., eds., *Zaidu Zhang Ailing* [Re-reading Eileen Chang]. Jinan: Shandong Pictorial Publishing House, pp. 20–31.
Xiao, Hong. 2002. *The Field of Life and Death & Tales of Hulan River*. Trans. Howard Goldblatt. Boston: Chen &Tsui Company.
Yan, Haiping. 1993. "Male Ideology and Female Identity: Images of Women in Four Modern Chinese Historical Plays." *Journal of Dramatic Theory and Criticism* fall: 61–81.
　2010. "Turning Points: Women Playwrights in Contemporary China." *Theatre Journal* 62.4: 519.
Yang, Lan. 2012. "Tian Qinxin: Women Are Like Drama, and Drama Is Life." www.youtube.com/watch?v=FajftD7J2WE, accessed on March 17, 2023.
Yang, Yi and Seokmin Yoon. 2023. "The Popularity of Korean Romance Novels in Contemporary China: A Feminist Interpretation." *The Journal of Popular Culture* 56.3–4: 689–703.
Yi, Shuo. 2011. "Huaju Sishitongtang chongxian jingdian" [*The Yellow Storm* Revives a Classics]. The Ministry of Culture and Tourism of the People's Republic of China. www.mct.gov.cn/whzx/zsdw/zggjhjy/201111/t20111121_776237.htm, accessed March 23, 2024.
Yu, Hongmei. 2013. "Visual Spectacular, Revolutionary Epic, and Personal Voice: The Narration of History in Chinese Main Melody Films." *Modern Chinese Literature and Culture* 25.2: 166–218.
Yu, Shiao-Ling. "To Revenge or Not to Revenge? Seven Hundred Years of Transformations of *The Orphan of Zhao* (2005)." *Chinopeal* 26.1: 129–47.

Zhao, Zhenjiang. 2015. "Zhuanfang Tian Qinxin: bie bei xifang jishu kongzhile, yao zuo weida de zhongguo wenhua"[Interview with Tian Qinxin: Don't Let Western Technology Control Us, We Must Create Great Chinese Culture]. Pengpai News. www.thepaper.cn/newsDetail_forward_1411666, accessed on September 13, 2024.

Zhang, Hong. 2012. "'Zhang Ailing re' sanshi nian weiceng lengque" [The Eileen Chang Fervor Hasn't Cooled in 30 Years]. Southern Art. www.zgnfys.com/m/a/nfrw-18123.shtml, accessed May 15, 2024.

Zhang, Lujing, 2010. "Zhong wen haishi zhong shang? Huaju shengsixian shang de neizhan" [The Civil War of Spoken Drama: Art or Commerce?]. *Zhongguo jingji zhoukan* [China Economic Weekly] 14: 16–18.

Zhang, Xiao. 2024. "'Su di chunxiao': yici zhongguo yanju jingshen de quanmian shijian" [Dawn at the Su Causeway in Spring: A Comprehensive Practice of the Spirit of Chinese Theater]. Guanghua ruiping [Guanghua Review]. https://ghrp.cctv.com/2024/04/06/ARTITkAc0o7h7FoxLnKVAxxp240406.shtml, accessed on June 23, 2024.

Zhou, Yu and Huang Qianning. 2013. "Tian Qinxin: nvren ru xi, xi ru rensheng" [Tian Qinxin: Women Are Like Theatre, and Theatre Is Life]. *Nanfang ribao* [Nanfang Daily], July 27.

Acknowledgments

This book grows out of my long-standing research interest in contemporary Chinese theatre, following the publication of several articles on main-melody plays, campus drama, and comedy.

I am deeply grateful to the editors of the *Women Theatre Makers* series, Elaine Aston and Melissa Sihra, for their guidance, encouragement, and generous support in bringing this book to fruition. My thanks also go to the team at Cambridge University Press for their prompt communication, technical assistance, and careful editorial work.

I am especially grateful to Brad Kent, who invited me to present part of this project at Université Laval during my academic visit to Montreal. The exchange with him and his wonderful students was both stimulating and encouraging. I also thank Feng Wei at Shandong University for his expert advice on Chinese traditional opera, a rich source from which Tian Qinxin draws extensively.

Finally, I owe special thanks to my husband, Tim Beaumont, for his patience and invaluable help with the manuscript.

For Tim and Danny

Cambridge Elements

Women Theatre Makers

Elaine Aston
Lancaster University

Elaine Aston is internationally acclaimed for her feminism and theatre research. Her monographs include *Caryl Churchill* (1997); *Feminism and Theatre* (1995); *Feminist Theatre Practice* (1999); *Feminist Views on the English Stage* (2003); and *Restaging Feminisms* (2020). She has served as Senior Editor of Theatre Research International (2010–12) and President of the International Federation for Theatre Research (2019–23).

Melissa Sihra
Trinity College Dublin

Melissa Sihra is Associate Professor in Drama and Theatre Studies at Trinity College Dublin. She is author of *Marina Carr: Pastures of the Unknown* (2018) and editor of *Women in Irish Drama: A Century of Authorship and Representation* (2007). She was President of the Irish Society for Theatre Research (2011–15) and is currently researching a feminist historiography of the Irish playwright and co-founder of the Abbey Theatre, Lady Augusta Gregory.

Advisory Board

Nobuko Anan, *Kansai University, Japan*
Awo Mana Asiedu, *University of Ghana*
Ana Bernstein, *UNIRIO*, Brazil
Elin Diamond, *Rutgers, USA*
Bishnupriya Dutt, *JNU, India*
Penny Farfan, *University of Calgary, Canada*
Lesley Ferris, *Ohio State University, USA*
Lisa FitzPatrick, *University of Ulster, Northern Ireland*
Lynette Goddard, *Royal Holloway, University of London, UK*
Sarah Gorman, *Roehampton University, UK*
Aoife Monks, *Queen Mary, London University, UK*
Kim Solga, *Western University, Canada*
Denise Varney, *University of Melbourne, Australia*

About the Series

This innovative, inclusive series showcases women-identifying theatre makers from around the world. Expansive in chronological and geographical scope, the series encompasses practitioners from the late nineteenth century onwards and addresses a global, comprehensive range of creatives – from playwrights and performers to directors and designers.

Cambridge Elements

Women Theatre Makers

Elements in the Series

Emma Rice's Feminist Acts of Love
Lisa Peck

Women Making Shakespeare in the Twenty-First Century
Kim Solga

Clean Break Theatre Company
Caoimhe McAvinchey, Sarah Bartley, Deborah Dean and Anne-marie Greene

#WakingTheFeminists and the Data-Driven Revolution in Irish Theatre
Claire Keogh

The Theatre of Louise Lowe
Miriam Haughton

Ellen Terry, Shakespeare, and Suffrage in Australia and New Zealand
Kate Flaherty

Performing Female Intimacy in Japan's Takarazuka Revue
Nobuko Anan

Feminist Imagining in Polish and Ukrainian Theatres
Ewa Bal, Kasia Lech

Caryl Churchill's Eco-Socialist Feminism
Elaine Aston

Lauren Gunderson and Feminist Theatre in the Twenty-First Century
Noelia Hernando-Real

Chinese Feminisms and The Vagina Monologues
Yingjun Wei

Adaptations in the Life and Work of Director Tian Qinxin
Yuan Li

A full series listing is available at: www.cambridge.org/EWTM

For EU product safety concerns, contact us at Calle de José Abascal, 56–1°,
28003 Madrid, Spain or eugpsr@cambridge.org.

www.ingramcontent.com/pod-product-compliance
Lightning Source LLC
LaVergne TN
LVHW011855060526
838200LV00054B/4344